MIRACLES
Expect Something Wild

25

Inspirational True Stories
of God's Unbridled Power

CONNIE BRYSON

constant byword

MIRACLES: *Expect Something Wild*
25 Inspirational True Stories of God's Unbridled Power
(The Art of Charismatic Christian Faith Series)
Written by Connie Bryson

Kindly direct all inquiries about this book to:
constantbyword@aol.com

Excepting brief excerpts for review purposes, no part of this book may be reproduced or used in any form without written permission from the author.

Except as otherwise noted, all Scripture quotations are taken from the New American Standard Bible ® Copyright © 1960, 1962, 1963, 1968,1971,1972, 1973,1975,1977,1995 by The Lockman Foundation used by permission. (www.Lockman.org)

ISBN 13 - 9780692247754 ISBN 10 - 0692247750

Copyright © 2014, Connie Bryson, all rights reserved.
The photos on the front and back cover of this book
© 2014, Photographer, Connie Bryson, all rights reserved.

Published in the United States of America

First Edition 2014

Acknowledgments

With my deepest appreciation, I thank all of the people who had a part in these true stories and for their openness to allow God into their lives and experience His power.

Thank you to my sons—who have made my life worth living, and my life complete. To Peter—for helping in bringing me back to God. To Lauren—for her encouragement, and for making me laugh. To my entire family. To my sisters—we made it through together. To Darlene—for the time she stepped in to protect me. To my parents, who miraculously rallied back. To my Uncle Sam—for taking me to church that night. To Susan, Martha, Diane, Michael, Lani, and Suzanne—who were there for me. To all the women who have attended my Bible study over the last twenty-seven years. Most of all—thank you, sweet Trinity—for all the miracles to be shared with all who have ears to hear.

Most names and some non-essential elements in this book have been changed in order to protect their privacy.

To my sons

I dedicate this book of amazing miracles to my two treasures, Joshua and Stephen. Motherhood has been the best part of my life. My sons have given me happiness I never had, and love I could never imagine! By being their mother, I developed a new perspective on life and its meaning. I am so proud of the wonderful, wise, and giving people that they have become. I love my sons more than words can express!

TABLE OF CONTENTS

PREFACE	11
INTRODUCTION	15
CHAPTER ONE *Voyage into Darkness*	27
CHAPTER TWO *The Multiplication of Easter*	35
CHAPTER THREE *Waiting for the Green Light*	41
CHAPTER FOUR *For my Ears Only*	51
CHAPTER FIVE *Both Gone*	55
CHAPTER SIX *My Two Treasures*	61
CHAPTER SEVEN *No Weapon Formed Against Him*	67
CHAPTER EIGHT *I Reached Up to God*	79

CHAPTER NINE 81
Seven Times for Skyler

CHAPTER TEN 89
The Phone Call

CHAPTER ELEVEN 97
There, Around the Corner

CHAPTER TWELVE 101
The Visit

CHAPTER THIRTEEN 107
The Great Escape

CHAPTER FOURTEEN 115
Faith Heals

CHAPTER FIFTEEN 119
Valentine's Day

CHAPTER SIXTEEN 123
Unfinished Business

CHAPTER SEVENTEEN 135
The Secret Behind 'Saved by the Bell'

CHAPTER EIGHTEEN 143
Nippy

CHAPTER NINETEEN 149
Princess Child

CHAPTER TWENTY 173
The Generator

CHAPTER TWENTY-ONE 179
The Dream that Came True

CHAPTER TWENTY-TWO 191
Comfort from a Painting

CHAPTER TWENTY-THREE 199
Brandon, We Love You

CHAPTER TWENTY-FOUR 205
Miracle by the Pool

CHAPTER TWENTY-FIVE 209
Jesus at the Gate

AFTERWORD 213

ABOUT THE AUTHOR 215

Preface

Amazing grace, how sweet the sound, that saved a wretch like me!

Oh, how I love that song. It brings comfort to me, as I kneel before an awesome God. One who is willing to hear from an ordinary person like me. He receives my heartfelt prayers, and listens to my cries.

He reached down and touched me in my brokenness, and made me whole. Every new day is a gift full of surprise, excitement, and endless love from my Father in Heaven. I humbly receive all that He has for me.

Once I gave my heart to God, He gave me a life that I could never have dreamed would come true—a life full of miracles in which I was blessed to play a part. It's a part that one can only grasp by embracing the gifts of the Holy Spirit, as Paul encouraged the church:

> *"Do not quench the Spirit; do not despise prophetic utterances. But examine everything carefully; hold fast to that which is good."*
> *1 Thessalonians 5:19-21*

Little did I know that God would gift me in a way that would profoundly affect others. Many of these miracles occurred during the final days of people's lives. What better time could God choose to intervene and show His grace and power, than at the moment of one's departure?

A servant of the Lord never boasts in herself, but only in the remarkable, supernatural power that comes from above. Just as the children of Israel encouraged one another by relating stories of God's miraculous interventions—the Lord asks us to remember and to share with others all that He has done in our lives. In that spirit, I humbly share these stories with you, stressing that it is God who deserves all the glory—and I, none.

The supernatural gifts of the Holy Spirit recounted in this book are listed in the Bible, in 1 Corinthians 12:7-11:

> *"But to each one is given the manifestation of the Spirit for the common good. For to one is given the word of wisdom through the Spirit, and to another the word of knowledge according to the same Spirit, to another faith by the same Spirit, and to another gifts of healing by the one Spirit, and to another the effecting of miracles, and to another prophecy, and to another the*

distinguishing of spirits, to another various kinds of tongues, and to another the interpretation of tongues. But one and the same Spirit works all these things, distributing to each one individually just as He wills."

It has been truly amazing to witness these extraordinary gifts, still in vital operation today.

The twenty-five true stories in this book are written simply, as they occurred. Great care has been taken to preserve the essential facts in each case.

I hope you will be touched by God, Himself, as you read about His unique ways and His undying love for each and every one of us. It's my prayer that you will be encouraged, and hopeful for experiences such as these to become manifest in *your* life.

Get ready to venture beyond your imaginings. Expect something wild!

My love to each reader,

Connie

Introduction

It was three minutes before four in the afternoon. I sat in my small office and stared relentlessly at my watch.

Beyond the French windows, I spotted Luke, my gardener, overwatering the newly planted pansies. Normally, I would have run, then skidded to a stop at the door to correct his over-zealous effort—but this time I sat quietly waiting.

Finally, it was four o'clock! I gently scooted my chair out from the desk, then ambled into the kitchen, as though someone were watching me. I didn't want to look too desperate. *Who was I trying to fool,* I thought.

I started humming to deter myself from feeling guilty while I poured a glass of white wine. I liked the dryer wines, the ones with a bit of a bite.

For several years, I had traveled to various places around the world to dine in the finest of restaurants. I'd indulged in the best of wines.

I hadn't always had an abundance. I grew up in Covina, California, in a tiny house with my parents and two sisters. This is where my life began.

In order to have more than one new dress for school, I had to babysit and do odd jobs starting at the tender age of ten.

My father was a WWII Veteran, who fought for our country at the age of seventeen. After the war, he worked as a quality control manager, inspecting parts for jets. My mother also worked odd jobs to help out. Eventually, she owned a small coffee shop in the corner of a market. She called it, *Sib's Corner.*

When I was young, my two sisters and I were playing on the patio that my dad had built. In those days, there were containers filled with sand that people would place around to extinguish their cigarettes in. They were called, "butt cans."

As I was skipping around the patio, I accidentally knocked over one of those cans. My dad, in a rage, came over and lined us up, and asked which one of us did it. My older sister, Darlene, knew that I would receive a terrible punishment, so stepped in, and said that *she* did it. She took the beating for me. I will never forget that act of love.

Sadly, my father became a mean drunk, which in turn made all of our lives difficult. My mother would also lose her temper at times. There were inappropriate beatings from both of them. This left no room for peace in our greatly dysfunctional household.

INTRODUCTION

With glass in hand, I gradually slipped back down into my chair and began to sip the wine. A small buzz came immediately. I seemed happier.

Realizing that I was relying on a drink to cover my sadness, I stopped. I became very still.

While gazing at the enticing drink, words echoed in my mind, fell to my lips, and escaped them: *"I'm either going to die—or I'm going to die."* Sounds awkward, but my life was in some way coming to an end, and I simply couldn't understand how.

My grandmother, Ida Golden, often told me stories about Jesus and occasionally read the Bible to me. She was my saving grace.

When I couldn't endure the atmosphere of my home, with a drunk father or a despaired mother, I would go visit Ida. What a comfort she was. She made me delicious food and would take me along to a meeting at her church. Ida was one of the founders and charter members of *The Assembly of God Church* in Covina. I had never known anyone who prayed and cried out to God with such fervency as she did.

One night, I stayed over with Ida. I'd been having lower back pain and couldn't sleep. We were cozy in her bed, as I laid on my tummy, facing away.

She started to pray for me when suddenly, I felt a large, warm hand on my back. It felt so good! I quickly turned my head to tell my grandmother that my back was healed. But to my surprise, she was sitting at the corner of the bed with arms raised up and praising God.

It wasn't *her* hand on my back—but God's.

Needless to say, I was healed. Undoubtedly, this was the beginning of a faith-building process.

My parents tried to walk a clean line with God, yet unwittingly yielded to the distractions and temptations of the world. They couldn't quite hold to the straight and narrow for long. As their hearts and minds became feeble, they slipped away from our familiar church to find another one where they weren't known.

Although my sisters and I felt the brunt of this, we made great efforts to find a haven, somewhere to hide ourselves to survive—even if it were a place in our own imaginations.

How did I end up sitting at this desk alone, drinking and feeling despaired? I am one who tried hard to survive in very painful environments, but found that I couldn't do it alone. I didn't have good morals or values instilled into my heart by parents, and kept trying to make everything okay. I somehow survived the challenges and hardships of the "evil teenage years." We moved to Claremont near the colleges in the middle of my Freshman year. I was thirteen when I enrolled into Claremont High School. Changing to another school would be difficult, but there were many new opportunities. The institution was known for its college preparedness.

My Uncle Sam lived a block away from us. He and his wife, Miriam, invited me to go to church with them one night. I was fourteen, and perhaps wanted to get out of the house, so I accepted their invitation. I jumped into an *A-line* dress (for those of you older than fifty), teased-up my hair while using half a can of hairspray (again, for those of you older than fifty), and waited for them to pick me up.

Promptly, they arrived with giant smiles on their faces, which made me cranky. I didn't like it that they felt so proud to have talked me into church.

Aunt Miriam asked me to go to the bathroom and look in the mirror and tell her what I saw. To my embarrassment, all I could see was black eyeliner encircling my blue eyes. We had to leave, though, so the make-up went with us.

I felt hesitant to go, but because I loved my Uncle Sam and didn't want to disappoint him, I climbed into the back of his station-wagon.

Arriving, I was a little nervous, a little convicted, and a little uncomfortable. We slid into a pew toward the back of the small sanctuary which made me feel more at ease. I was hoping to be invisible, but the pastor looked right at me as he welcomed the tiny crowd. *I've been spotted!*

The pastor preached, but I didn't hear a word. Memories of my life kept surfacing. I was desperately trying to escape them, but couldn't. I kept clicking my heels together, as though I was Dorothy in *The Wizard of Oz*—as she was also trying to escape.

At the end of the service, even with all of my fears and reservations—I found myself responding to the altar call. I knelt down at the stage and started to repeat a prayer the pastor was leading those of us being *led to the slaughter*, so-to-speak.

To my great amazement, I felt differently after receiving Jesus into my heart. It seemed as though someone had taken a bar of soap and scrubbed all of my insides clean. Especially around my heart.

We piled back into the car, and all I could think of was how refreshed and peaceful I felt.

Back at home in my pink bedroom, I fixed my eyes upon the wall with hidden hopes that I would see Jesus. *My grandmother saw him before, so maybe I will now. Or maybe I'll speak in tongues like she does.*

INTRODUCTION

The night closed before my quests came about. I didn't know what to do with my experience.

My uncle moved up to Northern California soon after our night together at church. No one was around to explain to me what had just happened and how to start a new life with God.

I developed a severe infection after a young man refused to take no for an answer. It turned into years of female-related health problems. This became a continual reminder of my past. A past full of darkness, hatred, and injustice.

Months went by, and I didn't go to church with my family. I didn't want to. At that time, I could never have imagined that it would take me fourteen more years to come back.

After high school, I went to work with my cousin, Janie, in Whittier, while taking night classes at college. After Janie got engaged, it was time for me to move back to Claremont, where I got a job as a salesgirl in a dress shop.

I was seventeen, and ready for adventure. My downfall was that I searched for love in ways that brought great loss to my life.

A short time later, I became a model and actor. All of my interviews were in Los Angeles, so I moved to Santa Monica at the age of nineteen. It was a little challenging at first, but I liked it.

After a few months, I had four national commercials on my resume. I was ready to begin an adventurous life away from parents and family.

Years later, I bought a home and wanted to settle there forever. An English Tudor with a flair of contemporary. A large plot of land and a great family home. *But where was the family?*

I glanced out the window to see Luke packing up his truck. I stopped drinking the wine and decided to exercise. On my brisk walk, I thought to call and make an appointment with my gynecologist. I was having more female problems and felt I needed to check it out. The doctor's answer to my problem was to put me on birth control.

My days became long and lonely. I was getting depressed and started to drink wine once again. One night after two glasses, I was waiting to hear back from my doctor. I had called and left a message describing the pain that I was having. He called me back and prescribed a glass of wine. *Hmm!*

I settled in the den, poured another glass of wine, and promptly answered the phone. It was an old friend of mine, Trudi. "Connie, I'm here with Peter, the television producer I told you about. He said he has a prayer for you."

Hastily, I replied, "Oh, give me a break!"

She answered quickly, "We'd like to come over so he can pray for you."

Everyone had known what a hard time I was having. I knew that Trudi was just trying to help, but I was not in the mood for this—yet suddenly—I asked, "How far are you away?" Without a breath, Trudi answered, "Three minutes. We're on our way!"

I sat on the sofa and wondered how this happened. *Why did I say it was okay for them to come? I look terrible. I don't want company!*

The doorbell rang. I swung open the door and a sense of soundness came over me. Peter had a wide smile on his face, and wore a baseball cap. Trudi, also had a smile, and wore an eager look. We went into the den and got comfortable. Peter then asked me a question: "So, how's your life?"

I was surprised, and thought his question was odd, personal, rude, and superficial. Offended, and yet replied, "I just want what Jesus wants!"

At once, I felt the earth's weight come off my shoulders. I was elated with joy and peace, as Peter leaned over to Trudi and whispered, "I thought you said this would be hard!"

Peter was a new believer and had quite an experience just a year before we met. He is Jewish, but only went to temple as a child and had no practicing faith for many years. But when he physically died and Jesus brought him back—he became a Jewish believer in Christ.

I received the Lord into my life that night and knew that *this* time it was for real, sincere, and eternal. Every aspect of life changed tremendously. The Lord came into my heart, while forgiveness flowed out of my heart—to *all* who ever hurt me.

The words I had said months ago, came back to me with understanding this time: *"I'm either going to die, or I'm going to die."* I now understood that I needed to die to sin and my old nature—and become alive in Christ. I never drank alcohol again.

Not long after my commitment, my mother and father re-dedicated their lives to the Lord. For all the years from that time until they went to Heaven, we enjoyed one another immensely. My mother's last words to me before she died were:

"Connie, I love you very much!"

Throughout my life, I was very maternal, but hesitated to have children. But now I wanted more than anything to have a family. I thought that perhaps I could adopt since I wasn't married.

But a year later, I did marry Peter. After being very close friends, we felt that the Lord was bringing us together for *His* reasons. I was excited to see what God was going to do in our lives. I knew this marriage would last.

Many things happened during the years of our marriage. My two treasures, Joshua and Stephen, were born—which made me the happiest woman alive. I loved motherhood more than anything else. I also gained a darling step-daughter, Lauren—who was Peter's daughter from a previous marriage.

Peter and I were blessed with the television show, *Saved by the Bell*, as well as many other shows for pre-teens and teenagers.

We held Bible studies at our home, and baptized believers in our pool.

We had a very full life with many activities. I always loved to paint oils on canvas, so when my sons were older and in school all day, I found an art studio to create in. I was blessed to sell many paintings and showcased my work in galleries nationally. God has used my art many times to bless others in very unusual ways.

These were the years when most of the following stories took place. What a great season!

And then, heartbreakingly—divorce. It came just short of twenty years.

You may be wondering why you would read a book that is written by a woman with a tainted past.

A woman with faults and failed relationships. If you're anything like me, I hope this book will encourage you that it's not about your failings. It's not about your sin. It's about the amazing grace of our God who forgives us, loves us, and uses us anyway.

How did I develop a close relationship with God? The more that I have been forgiven—the more that I have loved. I deeply appreciate that Jesus died for my sins. I was truly born again. My old self died and I became a new creature in Christ. I yielded to Him and wanted to know Him personally.

The stories you are about to read are all true and there were witnesses to all of them. I am sharing them so that others will have the chance to see God's undying love for all. Even a sinner like me.

God gifts believers like you and me—not according to how many great things we have done—but according to the condition of our hearts and our yieldingness to Him. I give all the glory to God. I love Him with my whole heart and have passionately devoted my life to Him. I am sincerely content with that. And I believe He is too.

I pray that these stories will touch your heart and create a desire there to draw closer to Him and to be used by Him greatly!

CHAPTER ONE

Voyage into Darkness

This story is written in memory of my father, Henry Garrison

Who could have imagined that it would take a trip downward into the deepest darkness to save my father's life?

It began with a desperate prayer that streamed out of a broken heart. The events leading up to this voyage started on our summer vacation.

Balboa Beach attracts all ages of people, especially those who love broad, sandy beaches with steady, consistent waves. The three mile strand which separates the beach from the harbor, includes Balboa Fun Zone. There in the village, stands the brightly-colored Ferris-wheel and a ferry that carries you across the bay. You can smell cotton-candy at every corner, as well as other special treats. My family had vacationed there a few times and were, once again, planning to go back for our upcoming summer break.

My sister, Alva, and I were nineteen months apart and shared a room in our small house in Covina. Being close in age, we were naturally competitive—both of us igniting ongoing debates.

The debate on one particular day was to decide which one of us would get the best room in the old, wooden beach house in Balboa. This time, though, our mother would not be there to mediate.

My parents were separated. My father had a drinking problem which was birthed in Okinawa, Japan, during World War II. This, among other issues, was the main reason they were divorcing.

Bob, my older sister's boyfriend, was calling for us to hurry and get into his car. The baby-blue '53 Chevy was warmed up for our trip, where we would meet with our dad.

Bob loved old cars, and quite frankly, it was the only kind he could afford. Alva and I would mercilessly beg to ride in it, as though it were a carriage for a princess. We also dearly loved Bob like a brother—and to our delight—he married Darlene years later.

We pulled up to the cabin in the *Baby-Blue,* and as we were getting our luggage out of the trunk, we saw Dad waving in the distance.

"Hey, you're here! Come on and hurry so we can get some sun before lunch," he shouted excitedly.

It seemed a bit odd entering the familiar cabin without our mother. But I had missed Dad. A warm and cozy feeling inside prevailed over the sadness. I couldn't wait to have quality time with him.

As always, I was hungry, so grabbed some chips and went through the cabin to the front porch. It was great to plop into the wonderful old rocker we all loved to sit in and view the ocean.

Dad looked good. Thin, and showing a tan. He took time to hug each of us, and I breathed-in the familiar scent of Coppertone he faithfully used. The excitement of summer hung in the air.

We kept busy that day, so I hardly had time to miss mom. But once evening arrived, and I was tucked into my bed, I missed her. I couldn't stop thinking of my parents, which interfered with my sleep. But it was more than my anguish that kept me awake. I was coming down with a fever and a depleting flu.

Why is this happening on the first night of our vacation?

I was too sick to join in with the others, so I stayed in bed. The next day brought along a higher fever, and Darlene started to worry. What I didn't know—was that a greater concern was at hand.

In the early morning, around 2:00 AM, Darlene came into my room and sat on the edge of my bed.

"Connie, wake up, honey. We need to go," she whispered.

Leaning in closer, she said, "Dad doesn't know we're leaving. He's been drinking and is drunk, so we are sneaking out in the night so he doesn't see us."

I miserably wretched with dry-heaves all the way home. It wasn't only from my flu. In some way I felt that we betrayed my dad.

The sun was starting to show itself above the roof of our home as we pulled into the driveway. Mom was fast asleep, so we tip-toed to our rooms and got into our beds. Darlene hurried to bring me some aspirin as she saw Bob off at the door.

For weeks, I pondered over what had happened. Feeling confused, I didn't know where to turn, except to God, Himself.

I remembered that my grandmother's church hosted a service every Wednesday night. I arranged to meet with her there. She was delighted that I was coming, but now I had to get a ride.

"Mom, can you take me to grandma's church tonight and pick me up when it's over?" She didn't answer right away, but finally said *yes*.

My grandmother lived in a small, white duplex directly behind the church. As I walked up her path, I could smell the carnations that were planted along each side of her front steps. I rang the bell and sang, "Grandma, it's me!"

She barely cracked the door to regretfully tell me that she sensed a cold coming on. She encouraged me to go ahead to the service without her. I felt a little shy going by myself, but so desperately wanted for God to help me. I walked into the church and found a seat by an open window. I glanced outside to see quite a crowd parking their cars.

To my surprise, the church was performing a play. I became enthralled in the theme and found myself wanting to be like the woman playing the role of a young housewife. She was beautiful and wore a soft-beige cashmere sweater with a black pleated skirt. She looked so grown-up.

During the last scene of the play the actors were disappearing from their homes and offices.

The Rapture!

My mind traveled immediately to my father. *Oh, Lord, don't let him go to hell! Please save his soul so that he will be with all of us!*

As I looked up through tears, my pulse raced to see that at least twelve adults had encircled me. It was when I felt the warm, caring hand of the woman that was in the play rest gently on my shoulder, that I relaxed.

The woman lovingly looked into my blurred eyes and asked, "What can we pray for you?"

In between sobs, I pronounced that my daddy needed to be saved, and asked:

"Please pray that he will stop drinking beer."

It was uncomfortable at first when they started praying, but soon after, I felt peaceful.

Once the prayers ended, I heard the subtle sound of brakes outside the window. Looking up, I saw my mom in her car. I dismissed myself while thanking everyone who prayed for my dad.

During the car ride home, silence settled between us. I dared not tell my mom of what had happened, knowing her response would be a negative one. I couldn't wait to tell my sisters what had occurred. But once we arrived at the house, I found Alva had gone to bed, and that Darlene had gone out with Bob.

Sleep was generous to me that night. I awakened early, hearing my name. I opened my eyes, and there was my dad!

"Dad," I said with surprise, "How did you get into the house?"

"The front door was unlocked," he answered.

My dad had no knowledge of what had happened in church the night before. He knelt down beside my bed and spoke these words:

> *"Connie, I promise you that I will never drink again. I promise that I will never lie to you again." My eyes welled up with tears as he continued: "Last night, Jesus took me by my hand and led me down a steep road into hell. There in its midst, He said to me, 'Henry, this is where you are going if you do not repent and come to Me.' Connie, I knelt before Jesus and received Him as my Savior and Lord. I am a new creature in Christ now—and you'll see that I've changed!"*

I sat up and hugged my dad. I told him what had happened in church—we both wept.

My dad certainly did change. Alcohol never touched his lips again. The Lord saved him from eternal death because of the prayers of a twelve-year-old girl and twelve loving adults—who truly had personified the love of Christ that night in church.

Once the divorce was final, my mom and dad started to date. They remarried one another a year after our "Balboa experience," and stayed happily married until death, did they part.

CHAPTER TWO

The Multiplication of Easter

Let me take you back to a season of glory. A time when God touched me in a way that changed my life. A time I will treasure forever.

I'd like to share with you about two astonishing supernatural experiences that blessed me in a way I could never have imagined. It was a time when many miracles were being made manifest within our household. A time of God's expressed love and generous provision.

It was early in the morning, as I stretched under the warm, cozy blankets. I glanced over at my clock which faithfully confirmed that Easter Sunday had arrived—I was to be baptized today!

Before long, I was driving through the majestic hills of California where they cascaded down to meet the ocean-side. At a secluded spot on the beach, my church was having an Easter sunrise service which included baptisms for all new believers.

Excitement embraced me, as I neared the shore. The sound of crashing waves greeted me, as the morning light began to glow. The brisk air brought a breeze which lifted my long hair so that it danced delightfully.

This is my day! Oh, God, thank you!

My life had been a torrent of difficult events and relationships—but now I was about to be adopted by God, Himself, and a new family who loved me just the way I was.

My parents and some friends came to celebrate. Some doubted this new-found faith of mine, but nothing could steal my joy.

I jumped from my jeep onto the soft-laden sand of Santa Monica, ready to venture into my new life with Christ. It all seemed perfect to me until my feet met with the cold waters of the ocean.

Where's the wet suit?

My pastor and his assistant held me arm-in-arm while waiting for the next wave. Suddenly, they lowered me into the frosty water before I had time to hold my nose.

Upon coming up from the sea, my arms flew up toward heaven. All of those on the shore thought in one accord:

Oh, look! Out of jubilation, she threw her arms up to praise God!

Little did they know that I had just swallowed half of the Pacific Ocean along with its sand—and was desperately trying to breathe again.

A few moments later, I became immersed in peace instead of water. I walked away from the small crowd to have a moment alone with the Lord.

I wasn't cold anymore, as I felt a blanket of God's warmth wrapped around me. There was a presence that I had never sensed before. I collapsed to my knees with great emotion.

Looking upward, I watched the bright-orange sun appear over the cliff. While admiring the beauty of the sunrise, I heard a voice coming from the heavens, out-loud:

"Connie!"

So soft and yet so bold. So loving and yet so powerful—*The voice of God!*

It was as though He said, *"My daughter, you've come home,"* all in one word.

I knew at that moment, I was His. That I would never leave Him, and that I would always serve Him.

A few years passed, and another glorious Easter Sunday had arrived. I invited my family and a couple of friends over for dinner to celebrate this special day. But little did I know, my husband had made an announcement at our Bible study the week before. He had openly invited everyone who didn't have a place to go for Easter dinner, to join us at our home.

I diligently arranged the dining room table with delightful little goodies, such as chocolate surprises nestled in tiny baskets. I busied myself, pacing between the kitchen and the den, where our uniquely small group of twelve guests were comfortably awaiting my call for dinner.

Glancing at the very tiny rolls, I wondered if I had enough. There had been a shortage of bread at the markets leaving a minuscule selection. The limitation allowed me to purchase a small package of bite-size rolls. I could only hope there would be enough for each of our guests. I was feeling fairly confident with the quantity of the other dishes until the doorbell rang. I wondered who this could be.

I waltzed to the front door and peered out the peephole. My jaw dropped, as I saw a line of people starting from the front steps, trailing along our brick pathway, and reaching to the sidewalk. I quickly counted them. There were twenty people!

How was I going to feed them all?

I froze a smile on my face and opened the door to greet them. "Welcome everyone! Make yourselves comfortable, we'll be eating soon," I repeated to each group of five.

Rushing back into the kitchen, I began to pray for a multiplication of food. Afterward, I called the troops in and each stood patiently in the lengthy line of ravenous guests. *This is when the miracle took place.*

I watched in amazement while each person took an abundance of food. My astounded husband told me that he was carving an *endless* ham.

And about those dinner rolls? No one took just one. I gasped to notice several of the men taking four or five each. Even the women took at least a couple. How could there possibly be enough for everyone? The guest count far exceeded the roll count on the package. But we never ran out.

Glory to God! He multiplied the food!

Everyone had plenty of each dish and there was food left over. Our God is the same yesterday, today and forever. I called upon the faithful Lord, and He generously answered my cry.

> *Lord, You are a God of miracles, and You will always perform them, as long as we yield and believe. Thank You for increasing our food—and my faith. Lord, may You hear and answer my prayers again and again, for your glory!*

CHAPTER THREE

Waiting for the Green Light

To think God would use a simple, normal person as myself, to perform such an amazing miracle! I had a lot to learn as a new believer and found myself making mistakes in the process. My heart had been leading me, so I had to make sure that my heart was in line with God's will and supernatural guidance.

God's timing is perfect, yet we can go before that timing and interfere with His divine plan. But as I grew from drinking milk to eating solid food, the mystery of *Spirit-filled living* began to reveal itself more clearly to me.

Balance is essential in our lives. When we can grasp that slippery fence of in-between, we can stand on solid ground without wavering. This lesson comes with many mishaps, but also with a reward that is everlasting.

Patience has never been my gift, but during the ongoing circumstances of fierce trials in my life, I've realized the great value of it. It is a priceless asset to covet and my journey has proved this to be true.

In our home, there were many interesting rooms. One, which we called *the green room*. There was a lovely hunter-green that married with other colors as it weaved its way through the burlap on the walls. Hunter green was also the color of fabric that dressed the sofas.

In most studios, where television and movies are filmed, there is a room where actors wait to be called onto stage. It's called *the green room*. But we used *our* room for prayer, and waited patiently for God's wonderful presence and answers—hence, the connection.

On an afternoon, I was reclining on one of the green sofas when I received a call from a friend I knew from church. Kyle was a musician who played guitar for the worship team. A quiet man, he stood around five feet eleven inches. He had a crown of straight, mellow-brown hair with blond highlights that were naturally applied by the Malibu sun. His face was tanned and embraced a wildly crooked smile that proved to enhance his character.

He informed me of a young woman in her thirty's named, Arlene, who had been diagnosed with a brain tumor. She was also pregnant.

Arlene was told two things. Firstly, she needed to undergo a very fragile brain surgery. Secondly, that she should abort the child in her womb.

Because of the type of pending surgery, there were threats of deformity and other serious side effects to the unborn baby.

Kyle asked me if I would go and pray for her.

All the things that I had been learning about using the gifts of the Holy Spirit were circling through my mind. "Kyle, this breaks my heart! I will seek the Lord for a day and see if God will direct me to go and pray for her."

Kyle was greatly disappointed with my response, but I didn't want to venture out into something I wasn't called by God to do.

I prayed sincerely for direction, and gracefully received it.

The Lord not only gave me peace, but showed me that Arlene and her baby would be healed!

The next morning, I called Kyle. "Can you meet me at the hospital? I'd like to go pray for Arlene," I eagerly stated.

Kyle was thrilled and gave me the information I needed to meet him in a couple of hours.

After strapping myself securely in my jeep, I was on my way. While waiting at the red light, I prayed that the Lord would give me a Scripture once I was there with Arlene. And upon my receiving it, I would know that God's anointing of healing would be present for her.

I parked my car and was on my way to meet Kyle. He anxiously greeted me and led me up to Arlene's room. Upon entering, I was surprised to see that there were so many guests—at least twelve. Some sat around the room in hard plastic chairs. Others stood in small groups chatting. I studied each one. Concern was on every face.

There, in the middle of the room, was Arlene. She seemed uncomfortable on the raised bed. Her face was pulled down on one side from the effects of the tumor. It took great effort for her to make a sound. She greeted me briefly as the surgeon entered. He also seemed surprised at the number of guests, but carried on with his work.

Seizing the opportunity, I asked the surgeon to show me the exact location of the brain tumor. He politely pointed, making a circle with his finger on the top of Arlene's head. I was grateful to have this valuable information so that when it came time for me to pray, I would know where to put my hand.

With Bible in place, I took a seat on a stool next to Arlene's bed. Hours went by while I watched her friends come and go as they gave their blessings to Arlene. She was set to have her surgery early the next morning.

I glanced at Arlene, and noticed her beautiful brown eyes and long lashes. Her skin seemed pale compared to her dark hair that was pulled back in a knot. The hospital gown seemed to fit her awkwardly, as she kept adjusting it.

Her husband, a young Swedish man with wavy hair and green eyes, made his way over to speak to Arlene. I glanced away, hoping to give them privacy.

Well into the next hour, the long-awaited Scripture finally came—from Arlene, herself. She spoke out slowly, drawing her words: "I almost forgot! My friend, Carrie, called earlier with a Scripture for me. It's Psalm 103:1-5."

With great enthusiasm, I opened my Bible and started to read the Psalm aloud:

"Bless the Lord, O my soul; And all that is within me, bless His holy name. Bless the Lord, O my soul, and forget none of His benefits; Who pardons all your iniquities; Who heals all your diseases; Who redeems your life from the pit; Who crowns you with loving kindness and compassion; Who satisfies your years with good things, so that your youth is renewed like the eagle."

The room became silent. Not a word was spoken. I was not the only one who felt God's presence. His glory was apparent and full of peace.

The healing power of God was present, and I was not going to waste a moment of it. *I had the green light!*

I gently placed my hand on Arlene's head, right over the place where the tumor was. Very softly, I prayed:

> *"Father, in the name of Jesus, I command this tumor to dissolve." I then placed my hand on Arlene's tummy and prayed, "I pray this baby will be born without any deformation or health issues whatsoever."*

I settled back onto my stool. The room remained hushed, as one-by-one shed silent tears. These tears were not from sadness or fear, but tears that came from being in the presence of the living God—who so lovingly visited us that hour.

The silence was broken when a young woman, wearing a red and white striped apron and carrying a clipboard, came in. She walked across the *glory-filled* room while asking for the husband of Arlene.

The young Swede jetted-up from his seat to claim the requested title.

The woman described the contents of the papers that Arlene's husband had to sign in preparation for the morning's surgery. Just as he was about to sign, I jumped off my stool and put my hand on his shoulder. "Please," I pleaded, "Don't sign the papers! Your wife is healed. I understand this is hard to believe, but I know God healed her. She doesn't need the surgery."

The young man looked wearily into my eyes and said, "You have to understand. I am not a believer like you and my wife. I have to sign this."

He turned and signed the papers.

My heart ached at the thought of Arlene going through brain surgery unnecessarily.

After retrieving my car, I was on my way home. The sense of victory battled with the disappointment of unbelief. I truly understood Arlene's husband's dilemma.

The next day, I called Kyle to get information on the outcome of Arlene's surgery. Kyle wasn't available, so I called the hospital and was told that Arlene had been released. *Released?*

Research books and concordances were stacked high on the kitchen table in orderly columns. I had set a day apart to compile my Bible lessons for the week. As I began to study, my phone rang. It was Kyle. "Kyle, where have you been?"

He sheepishly responded, "I had to leave for two weeks and I just got back."

I quickly put a post-it note in my book so I wouldn't lose my place, and asked, "Did you ever find out what happened to Arlene?"

After pausing, he responded, "Oh, my gosh! Didn't you hear?"

He began to tell me the story: "God healed Arlene just as you prayed! She went under surgery the next morning and all they found was dried up blood where the tumor had been."

I felt elated in my spirit and an enormous surge of exuberance, as I shouted upward toward the heavens: "Praise God!"

After Kyle and I profusely thanked God and praised Him for this miracle healing, I went out to my backyard to be alone with the Lord.

It was late morning with a hint of spring in the air. I could see a group of solid-white clouds forming together in the distance. Hummingbirds squealed in the garden. They performed acrobatics, flying upward at great speed—then suddenly dive-bombing down again.

A fluttering butterfly graced my presence. All of God's creation seemed to be rejoicing with me over Arlene. *Oh, how God loves His children!*

I slowly walked back into my home. Upon entering, I looked outside once more to the clouds. *The heavens declare your glory, Lord!*

I made a cup of tea steeped to perfection and seasoned liberally with milk and raw sugar. Through tears of appreciation, I spoke to God:

"Oh, my God, my Lord, how I love You! How I am in awe of your majestic character, your enormous kindness. I am moved by your grace and mercy. I am blessed by your eternal love. You have touched a family in their desperate hour. I now ask You to open up the heart of Arlene's husband, in Jesus' name."

One day, several months later, I heard the mail sharply hit the shelf of my mailbox. Within the bundle of many envelopes, a dainty, slight-pink one peeked out at me. The letter inside read:

Dear Connie,

I just found out your name. All I knew was that a very special person came into my hospital room, many months ago, and prayed for me. That person is you! As you know, my tumor was gone, as you had prayed it would be. The surgery was indeed unnecessary. But you also prayed for the baby in my womb that day. My doctors had pleaded with me to abort my child.

They said that without a doubt my baby would be deformed due to all of the medicines I had consumed, and from the surgery.

I have just given birth to a beautiful, healthy girl. I will never forget what you did for me and my family by being obedient to God. Also, my husband is now a believer.

love and appreciation forever,
Arlene

I folded the letter, placed it back into its envelope, while almost exploding with indescribable exultation. It was an expression of knowing God, who performs miracles through His children.

To Him be all the glory forever and ever!

CHAPTER FOUR

For My Ears Only

Oh, how I look back at my life with disbelief over the things I have done! *Smoking? How insane is that?*

We have enough problems with air quality, and yet some of us purposely drag on lit chemicals rolled in thin paper—to our demise.

I was twelve when I visited Loma Linda Hospital on a school field trip. There, we viewed a film showing the physical ramifications of smoking. The graphic video of a black lung turned me into an aggressive opponent of cigarette smoking.

My sister had been smoking for a couple of years and I was going to do any and everything in my power to stop her.

Shockingly, only a couple of years later, human nature and all of its downfalls challenged me. I fell into the same trap of self destruction. I certainly didn't practice what I had preached, and quickly became a victim of senseless substance abuse.

I was fourteen years foolish when I took my first puff. Call it peer pressure, boredom, or pure ignorance, I smoked off and on—until one day, the God of heaven brought it to a screeching halt.

Once I had committed to follow Jesus, I faced a daily battle to conquer this obnoxious habit. After trying everything in my human power to kick this in the butt (literally), I asked God for help.

I prayed, but my fleshly desires prevailed. One morning, as the phone awakened me, I lit a cigarette and began my conversation. My friend was speaking while I heard a bold, voluminous, audible voice, say:

"STOP SMOKING NOW!"

Immediately, I questioned my friend with great fervency. "Did you hear that?"

Innocently, she answered, "No. What was I supposed to hear?"

Again, I asked, "You mean, you didn't hear that? You had to have heard that!"

Again, she demanded, "Hear what?"

Then, I realized that she hadn't heard a thing, but that *my ears only* heard the voice of God. It was for me, not for her. I knew that God spoke out-loud to me and that He was serious about what He said. There were no doubts—I had to *stop smoking now!*

After my friend and I finished our conversation, I knelt by my bed and prayed:

"Dear Lord, I heard your voice and I know it was You. I can't stop smoking on my own, but with You, all things are possible. It has to be your strength working in me. I will yield to You. Please take away my desire and addiction."

I never desired to smoke again, or craved nicotine after this divine encounter. I give all the glory to God, who so gracefully gave me the strength to yield to His command.

CHAPTER FIVE

Both Gone

Traveling is a luxury for most people, but for me, it's a challenge. I'm not crazy about flying, and have had an uncanny number of "close calls" and situations of extreme danger in my travels. Many times, nearly facing death.

But how else will I get to places?

My two sisters and I planned a trip to visit our grandmother. Little did we know that this trip would become one of the most terrifying trips of our lives. My dad's mom was truly a character. Her humor was contagious and kept you feeling warmly connected. We visited as often as we could during our childhood years.

We had never spent Thanksgiving with grandma Mildred, so we thought it would be a great first. She was getting older and one never knows when the wind from heaven will swoop down and carry us up.

The flight out of Los Angeles would take us to St. Louis, where we would board another plane and head to Springfield.

Once we were up in the air, Darlene, Alva, and I began to reflect on all of the visits to Illinois throughout the years.

Our dad and mom would bravely drive us across the States in their old Chevy station-wagon, aware of the difficulties such a trip could hold. If one of us weren't saying we had to go to the bathroom again, the other was saying that chicken-pox were developing on her leg. These, and similar events, never seemed to cease.

It was both enjoyable and educational to travel and view this beautiful land, called America. The sunsets, turtles crossing the road, and flash-lightning kept us entertained until—"Daddy, please stop the car, we're hungry!"

Regardless the time of our arrival to grandma's house, there in the kitchen awaited a freshly roasted turkey, egg noodles, and hot apple pie. I have no recollection of my dad calling her from a telephone booth and was convinced my grandma simply had *grandma-insight*.

Once we landed in St. Louis, my sisters and I were longing for our next flight. We wondered why we weren't boarding our plane since we could see it out the window, ready to go.

When our flight was finally announced, we were led out a door into the cold air of the evening. We asked a pilot, who was walking our way, where we were going.

"To our plane. Come and follow me."

As we did, this confident, young air navigator walked around the jet we thought was ours, and proudly pointed to the tiniest plane I had ever seen at a commercial airport.

Alva said, "Oh no! I'm not getting on this *toy* plane!" With that, we all laughed hysterically as we forced ourselves to climb in. There were six seats including the two pilot's seats. It wasn't until the plane started up that we noticed the propellers.

No jet engines? Just two propellers?

My older sister, Darlene, and I were newly seated in the Body of Christ, but Alva hadn't committed her life to Christ yet. She asked us why we were so peaceful. Our answers were the same. "We have peace from the Lord."

We made it up into the air and I glanced out the window to see the beginning of snow. I was caught up in the beauty of it when a sudden shriek of metal loomed over me.

We all shouted in unison: "What was that?"

There was nothing but a frail yellow curtain between us and the two pilots. The co-pilot pulled the curtain back and answered, "We lost one propeller, but don't worry—the other one can take us down." *Easy for him to say, "Don't worry!"*

My right hand was losing circulation, as Alva's hand tightly clenched it. "Alva," I said, "Don't worry, we will be fine. The Lord will protect us."

Just when we were convincing Alva to calm down and relax, we were wildly distracted by another shriek.

Now, *I* was starting to fear from what I believed we would hear next. The co-pilot pulled back the curtain—this time to its fullest extension. A beeping sound almost made him inaudible, as he shouted, "We have now lost our other propeller!"

Oh joy! We are going to glide into Springfield on the snowy, wet ground. Meanwhile, we were somehow supposed to remain peaceful.

The beeping seemed louder every second as we three sisters huddled together with our eyes tightly shut. Darlene and I continued our prayers as Alva was giving herself her last rites.

But in the midst of this, a peace filled that tiny plane, as the snow drifted slowly and gracefully—and it seemed we followed in its path. Surreal as it appeared, we experienced the flight of a snowflake.

At once, we felt motionless and weightless. It was as though God placed His hand under the belly of our plane, guiding it gently down to earth. And now we were sitting on the runway as though we never touched it—Grandma in the distance waiving her arms, anxious to see us.

We didn't tell grandma what had happened until the third day of our visit. She was so grateful to God for delivering us to her by sparing our lives.

As we sat eating turkey and noodles, awaiting the apple pie, we knew the Lord had blessed us in a very unusual way. We toasted with our juice and looked up toward heaven and said:

"Thank you Lord, who triumphs over all, for loving us and giving us the most appreciated Thanksgiving ever!"

CHAPTER SIX

My Two Treasures

Hearing a devastating report about your health at a young age will challenge your faith. But when God shows up—anything can happen!

It was the month of March when I met Peter, and we married a year later.

June came quickly, as we were expecting a visit from Lauren. Peter had a daughter from a previous marriage, who would be staying with us the entire summer. I was looking forward to bonding with her.

We played games, spent a lot of time in the pool, and experienced heaps of laughter. We also started writing plays together and performed them for Daddy.

Although she was young, Lauren wanted to go to day camp. We signed her up, and the next week she was off in a small, mustard-yellow bus.

Some friends from church were coming over the following weekend, so I started to make my plans. I loved to entertain and enjoyed coming up with new recipes.

The weekend arrived and so did our guests. Our day included a seasonal lunch, swimming, warm conversations, and prayer in the late afternoon.

As we prayed that day, a kind, charismatic woman told me that God had given her a picture of my health. I had been having female problems and had gone to get checked out the month before. What my friend, Lisa, didn't know was that I had been diagnosed with endometriosis. The doctor told me that I had become completely sterile and would not be able to have my own children.

This news was hard to swallow, but I remembered God's promise to me about my sons. Not long before, when I committed my life to the Lord, He revealed to me that I would have two sons. They would be very close in age. One darker with brown hair and eyes—and the other, very blond with fair skin and blue eyes.

Lisa asked if she could pray for me. After I approved, she laid her hands gently on my abdomen and prayed. Lisa described the picture God had given her. It perfectly illustrated endometriosis.

After the prayer, I grabbed her with a hug and proclaimed, "I'm going to have my two sons!"

For the next couple of days, I felt as though I had a light bug of some sort. Maybe God's way of having me rest after such a healing.

Peter was working at home downstairs, and Lauren was at day camp. I was resting in bed when Peter came slowly up the stairs. I could see his shadow on the linen closet doors as he approached. He shyly peeked around the stairwell into the bedroom and asked, "Do you want to be together?"

As I considered his words, I heard a love-filled, inner voice say: *"You will now conceive a child."* That was it! Signed, sealed, and delivered. I knew I was pregnant and no one could tell me otherwise. God touched me and miraculously healed me.

As Peter started down the stairs to go back to work, he gave me a quick glance and very quietly spoke, "You know—you're pregnant."

Five minutes later, I was running down the stairs to the office where Peter was. "What did you say to me upstairs?"

He playfully answered, "You heard me."

Anxiously, I said to him, "You said I was pregnant. How did you know that?"

Now, with a larger grin, he answered, "Because, as I was working down here in my office, the Lord clearly said: *'Go be with your wife and she will conceive.'* "

I looked at Peter with widened eyes, and excitedly declared, "I'm pregnant! When you came upstairs, the Lord said to me:

'You will now conceive a child.' "

I thanked God, as my heart was full, and my mind raced with thoughts of all the wonderful years to come. That very moment, my life changed. I no longer cared about myself and my priorities, but turned my passion toward being a mother.

There was one huge test of faith that came with this blessing, though. The result from my blood work came back negative. The doctor said I wasn't pregnant. I continued to believe God's words. I told my doctor that God promised me this child. He gave me a number to call for a psychiatrist.

A home test proved that I was indeed pregnant. Joshua John was born. I was the happiest person alive. The second his tiny lips touched the air, he screamed out a loud cry. *I knew right then that his voice would be heard.*

Thirteen months later, I heard the whisper of the Lord, once again: *"Connie, you will now conceive your second child."*

That night, I conceived and was pregnant. My joy accelerated as the months sped along. Stephen David was born and I felt complete. Instead of a scream—a small, quiet yawn. *I knew immediately that my son was an over-comer.*

> *"Oh, Lord, I am at peace looking at my two treasures in my arms. One with dark skin, eyes*

and hair—and the other, blond, fair skinned, and with blue eyes. I have had my children now and I feel satisfied. I will raise them according to your Word. I ask for wisdom from above to prevail in each decision I make concerning them. I ask for knowledge to share with them to enable them to grow within. I ask for discernment in times of difficulty when trials arise. I thank You, Lord, with all that is within me for giving me the desires of my heart. I do not look upon this responsibility lightly, but I know that I can do well with your help."

CHAPTER SEVEN

No Weapon Formed Against Him

My heart pulsated wildly, as I sat fixated before my TV. The news was covering one of the most tragic murders of its kind.

I held my breath.

Many years ago, I developed a friendship with a very special person named Danny Franks. We met at his place of employment, in a well-known jewelry store in Southern California. Danny was both personable and charming, which contributed to his success at his job. His youthful smile was sweetened with a sincerity that welcomed even the most prestigious of customers.

Danny always had exciting adventures to share that he drew from his exotic travels. Starting with Nebraska to Calcutta and around the globe, he would eagerly look forward to every vacation throughout his tenure selling jewels.

We never missed the opportunity to laugh at our stories and at ourselves—But one day soon, the laughter would stop.

I hadn't seen Danny for a few years until he dropped by to introduce himself to my three-month-old son, Joshua. After an active game of paddle tennis with my husband, Danny was off again on another journey to a distant land.

I lost communication with him after a while, but always kept him in my thoughts. I pictured him on a secluded island viewing exquisite sunsets or in Saudi Arabia taking pictures of the wind-sculptured sand dunes. I prayed that God would continue to give him traveling mercies.

Now and then, I managed to schedule some time to paint while my son napped. My passion for oils on canvas drove me to keep my eager fingers on the brush.

I usually painted from photographs that I had taken of landscapes or cityscapes. One time in particular, an image came to mind. A young man barefooted and dressed in denim overalls, wearing a straw hat. He was sitting on marble steps which led up to a white stately building.

Towering columns were ensconced handsomely along the front terrace of the structure. There were bright-red flowers that circled the building on the edges of the freshly mowed grass. Several trees, all the same height—all in a straight line, were perfectly placed and perfectly spaced.

The young man was looking down at the ground seemingly in deep thought.

After seeing this image periodically for almost a year, I was convinced that God wanted me to paint it. As I sat at the easel, it came so easily.

Once the painting dried, I hung it in my bedroom. Though I grew fond of this painting, I knew it didn't belong to me.

I had been thinking of Danny, and heard through a mutual friend that he had married. This news brightened my day. I started to pray for him, then heard a soft voice within me say:

"Connie, pray for Danny—that no weapon formed against him shall prosper."

I knew this Scripture well. It's found in the Bible in the Book of Isaiah, chapter fifty-four, verse seventeen. Although this instruction from the Lord concerned me, I refrained from questioning it. I prayed with diligence the very words the Lord had spoken.

After two weeks of praying for Danny, a most devastating tragedy took place. A friend of mine called to inform me of the news. She said that a man was in the jewelry store where Danny worked, holding some employees hostage with a gun. She had just heard this report on the radio, but had few details.

It is almost impossible for me to express the pain I felt in my heart. I quickly sat on the floor of my exercise room for fear of fainting. I kept picturing Danny being killed, as well as my other dear friends: Ricky, Mindy, Lena, and Todd, the doorman.

We had developed a bond throughout the years during my visits to the store. And now, there they were—locked-up and awaiting their fates. As each of their faces came before me, I lifted them up in prayer.

Memories flashed before me. Danny and I riding bikes on the beach, our numerous lunches together, and riveting talks about God.

After a lengthy, tumultuous day, I finally learned of Danny's safety while watching the afternoon newscast. I later got more details from Danny, himself.

Danny was upstairs in an office at the time the intruder entered the store. Shortly afterward, he was headed downstairs to see if everyone was ready for the day, when he suddenly stopped—then froze. To his left, in an adjacent showroom, he saw a man holding a gun against Lena's head. He assumed Ricky, Mindy and Todd were in there, as well.

He stood in neck-deep fear as he pondered his move. If he tried to rescue these few, he could in-turn be killed, himself. But if he went back upstairs, he could get the other employees out of the building safely.

Cautiously, Danny moved up the stairs and commanded everyone to exit as quickly and quietly as possible. Once they were out of the building, he grabbed a phone and called the police. He then escaped while the police were on their way.

Danny was able to assist the authorities in calling the store to speak to the gunman.

Meanwhile, the policemen had arrived and started to approach the store. Ironically, their arrival threw the gunman into a panic.

The gunman declared on the phone that he had just shot and killed Lena.

Danny, with exasperation inexpressible, begged those in charge to be more careful—to not risk the others' safety.

A more sophisticated Los Angeles team was then called in to help. They positioned themselves all around the city with their weapons. It was quite an eerie image to watch on TV. Dreadful news came once again.

Todd had been brutally stabbed in the back by the intruder, and was killed.

The special team members stood close by, as the gunman inside the store gave orders. He commanded Mindy to gather the velvet fabric that draped the store windows and bind them together. Mindy reached for her sewing kit in her desk drawer.

Once the fabric was adhered, the gunman forced the surviving hostages under it, as they started outside into full view.

A moving blanket with shuffling feet below was headed for the parking lot where the gunman's car was parked.

Ricky, realizing there must be plenty of police surrounding them, pointed under the fabric toward the gunman. By doing this, he was hoping the police would see the position of the gunman, so that they could take a shot at him.

Tragically, a team member mistook Ricky's pointed finger for a gun, and shot and killed Ricky—thinking he was the gunman.

The impact lifted the blanket, which left them lying on the ground. The team was able to rush in and recover the last surviving hostage: Mindy.

The gunman was taken away, which left two innocent people. One sitting in hysteria—and one motionless. Dead.

Soon, they were gone too, and the store was flooded with police and team members to find the murdered bodies inside.

I couldn't sleep that night, as my mind played a re-run of the events, over-and-over again. I wanted to speak to Danny desperately, but knew I couldn't for at least a couple of days.

Losing these friends in such a violent, senseless manner took a fierce toll on me. My distress manifested into illness.

I awoke the following morning overwhelmed with nausea, along with a headache and exhaustion. I settled into bed to rest—which lasted for two weeks.

During my time of recovery, I composed a letter to Danny. I shared how God had directed me to pray for him, *"that no weapon formed against him shall prosper."* I also expressed how I believed that God spared his life.

The last day that I spent in bed, I studied the painting on my bedroom wall that God had inspired me to paint. I then asked a question. "Who is this painting for?" Promptly, I heard the Lord's loving voice say: *"This painting is for Danny."*

A few days later, I arranged to visit Danny. I parked in the parking lot behind the store, took a deep breath, and went inside. All new faces greeted me. None of them knew who I was.

One kind man informed Danny that I was there, then escorted me upstairs. My dear friend was sitting behind his desk, looking pale and depleted. I feared at that moment that he may never heal from this dark and evil experience.

We spoke for a while, then I asked him if he'd come down to my car, where a gift awaited him. He agreed and we were on our way. Entering into the lot, I realized that I was parked where Ricky had been shot and killed.

Approaching the car, Danny saw the painting in the back seat.

"Connie," he said, with a strong voice, "That's me! That's me in the painting! I'm always in the rose garden. There I am—sitting on the steps, waiting."

Danny covered his face with his hands, bent over, and wept. This was the first time that he was able to cry since the murders.

I opened the car door to grab the painting and placed it by his side. He hugged me, picked up the painting, and walked back toward the store with his head hanging low.

I knew not to say a word. There were no words to say. Danny had been moved tenderly by the painting that God asked me to paint and give to him.

Throughout the following days, I kept in touch with Danny to see how he was recovering. One morning, I prepared to read the newspaper and viewed a face I will never forget. There, on the front page, was a photograph of the gunman who shot and killed my friends. I felt weak and started to shake as I studied this man's face.

Oh my God!

I quickly called my pastor's wife, to see if she also recognized the young face. She picked up the phone, somehow knowing it was me, and cried out, "Oh my God, Connie! Did you see him?"

I replied, "Yes, Maggie, it's him—the young man!"

The night before the shooting at the jewelry store, I attended a Bible study at my pastor's home. Directly before the teaching began, I noticed a young man, perhaps in his early twenties, walk into the house. I sensed a darkness about him. I approached my pastor and whispered in his ear: "Something's very strange about that young man—I can feel death all around him."

Pastor James approached the man and asked him if he'd like prayer. The man declined and quickly left the meeting.

Looking down at the photo once again, I said, "My dear Lord! How could it be that the man who wandered into our prayer group that night—murdered my friends the next morning?"

My pastor's wife and I both agreed that this confused, sick person was subconsciously looking for the truth and for help.

Once our conversation was over and we hung up, I started to pray with a love that only God could have placed in my heart.

"God, forgive him," I cried, "He's sick! Have mercy on this man, Lord, and draw him to You, I pray."

The death sentence had been given to this gunman, but I had never heard of the final outcome of his demise.

Recently, I looked online to see if I could find the article that I so tenderly cried over that day, years ago. In my search, I found that this man started reading the Bible in prison and asked God to forgive him. Up to this date, he is still alive and has a redeemed relationship with God.

> *Oh, the mysteries of God! Who can know them? Who can think as He does? I have tried to understand His ways, but they are higher than mine. I don't know why my friends had to die. But I do know that prayer with a Scripture saved Danny's physical life, and prayer with a broken heart saved a murderer's spiritual life.*

It will always be a mystery to me, how an image that God gave me to paint touched Danny in a way that effected his life so profoundly. I do know that God knows—and that's all that matters.

CHAPTER EIGHT

I Reached up to God

There are times when we are forced to act on something quickly, even during an urgent moment when panic arises. It's quite distressful to witness your child in a helpless situation, let alone, in pain.

Visit with me to a time years ago when my firstborn son was two years old. Acting on faith alone enabled me to help him.

I had placed Joshua in his car seat, and we were on our way to do some errands. He loved shopping with me, and we always had fun playing games with the shopping cart. When we were finished marketing, I secured Joshua in his car seat again.

As I shut the car door, Joshua simultaneously moved his hand over into the way of contact. His precious little fingers were now crushed and jarred in the door. Immediately, he screamed from the enormous pain—and I panicked. *Oh, my God, what have I done?* Carefully, I opened the door.

My first thought was to grab Joshua, run back into the market, and get some ice on his injured fingers. But something made me stop, as though time stopped as well. Reaching down, I placed Joshua's throbbing hand into mine, while raising my other hand upward to Heaven. I prayed as only a mother could.

After my prayer, my courageous child brought his hand up to his face—in order to closely inspect it—and declared, "All better, Mommy!"

Now, it was my turn to inspect. There was no sign of injury, swelling, or broken fingers—a miracle!

> *When we take our faith and thread it into a frantic moment, we can receive a calmness along with a swift touch back from God. Not only was I grateful beyond words, my young son had experienced his first miracle. Oh, the joy of the living God! I reached my hand upward to God, and in turn, He healed my son's hand.*

CHAPTER NINE

Seven Times for Skyler

God works in mysterious ways, and at times with a miracle healing, defying all natural explanations. A young man with a promising future is suddenly caught up in a race against the clock, fighting for his life. But with God, things can change in a moment.

Wednesday nights always included a lot of preparation for the Bible study we hosted at our home. Around fifty people attended weekly. At that time, my son, Joshua, was an active and charming toddler at eighteen months old. His little brother, Stephen, was nestled in my womb.

It was the middle of autumn when we planned to have a baptism in our pool for the new members of our group. Being that cold weather had been flirting with us, we diligently prepared ahead and heated the pool for the event. My husband was planning on teaching that night, and afterward, conducting the baptism with the help of two others.

One of the new believers eager to be baptized, was nineteen-year-old, Skyler. His parents were very excited about the upcoming celebration. They were a Jewish family who believed in Jesus as their Messiah.

Sandy and John's only concern was for the health of their son. Not because they were doting parents, but because their son had cancer—a rare form of Leukemia. The doctors had recently informed Skyler, along with his family, that they weren't able to do a lot more to save his life.

A unique quality in Skyler's character caught everyone's attention. He was simply *loveable*. A thin, but muscular man with a trace of reddish hair that was left from the ongoing bouts of chemo. He wore a hat to hide his baldness, but exuded youthfulness with his charming, invigorating personality. With courage and determination, he never gave up on anything he believed in.

When we first announced the upcoming baptism at our home, Skyler was the first to respond and started planning his approach. He informed us that he wanted to go under the water seven times, as Naaman the leper did in the Bible, and afterward was healed.

As much as Skyler's ambition exhibited bravery, it also brought more concerns to his parents. They feared the effect of the chilling air, as well as the physical energy it would take for Skyler to be immersed numerous times.

The exciting event was approaching, when my husband got a call to go out of town for his work. It would be on the night of the planned baptisms.

I could feel my feet getting cold and my face becoming flushed. Normally, this wouldn't be a concern. But the idea of my having to do all the preparations, teaching and baptisms, was clouding my head. I looked down at my seven-month tummy and mumbled, "Oh, mercy!"

The next morning, I awoke early to get a headstart. It was cooler than usual with a wisp of mint in the air coming from our *Peter Rabbit's garden*. The smell was delightful, as I browsed around my garden gathering rosemary and thyme.

It was truly a task to bend down in my condition. I started to laugh, as I pictured God sitting in His throne room laughing sweetly along. A peace came over me and I was ready for the night's challenge.

After confirming my babysitter and the two men that would help with the baptisms, I prepared the lesson for the evening. *What else would I teach on, but healing?*

While organizing my lesson, I prayed for the night. I asked the Lord to honor Skyler's impressive faith by bringing forth healing soon after the seven-time-under baptism.

The number *seven* made its way quickly on my watch. It was time for the meeting. The first few people arrived and kindly volunteered to place the fold-up chairs around the room. *Always thankful for cheerful workers!*

Something stirred within me to suggest they put out ten more chairs than usual. It's a good thing I did, since sixty-five people showed up.

Skyler arrived early, along with bathing suit and towel. His childlike faith made me tear, as I pleaded to God for his safety. Trailing behind Skyler, came his parents and grandparents. I couldn't help but feel the frightful concerns of Skyler's mom—the agony of fighting through a son's illness. Her brow was tense and her eyes weary. I gave her a loving hug.

After the Bible study, the time came to venture outside into the frosty air and begin the baptisms. Thankfully, the moon was generous, and displayed a lovely, dancing gleam upon the steamy water.

As the men prepared to begin the baptisms, they were not surprised to see that Skyler was first in line. *Seven times under,* he went—as his mother gasped for air. *Seven times under,* he went—as the angels rejoiced in heaven. *Seven times under,* he went—with faith far greater than a mustard seed.

In a split-second, Skyler's parents were there at the top of the pool steps with towels. They rushed him into the house, dressing him quickly with dry clothes.

It was now done. Skyler's last effort for a miracle healing. I imagined that God was smiling down upon him.

The crowd flocked around our kitchen table which abounded with every kind of snack food and dessert you can imagine.

Someone tapped on my shoulder. I turned to see Skyler's parents. His father explained that they had been in a lot of prayer for their son, and believed they had an idea that would work. My curious ear egged him on as he spoke. "Skyler broke his collarbone as a child and it bumps up under his clothes. We've asked God to heal it tonight. If He does, then it would be a sign to us that Skyler's cancer will also be healed."

Oh, the love of parents!

I gently suggested that they should not expect the healing to happen this way. Yes, it would be great if God chooses to heal Skyler's collarbone as well—but we needed to wait upon the Lord for *His* answer.

When the babysitter and last friend left, I went upstairs to see my Joshua, who was fast asleep. While glancing down at him, I felt deep gratitude for this precious gift from God.

Once in my bed, I relived each part of the evening until I fell asleep. I awakened well-rested and excited about the dream I had just had. I knew that it was from God.

As I thought about the dream, Joshua and I enjoyed breakfast together. I was inundated with excitement, while awaiting a decent time to call Skyler and his family.

Once Joshua was ready for the day, I prepared to make my call. Skyler answered with anticipation in his voice: "Good morning!"

"Skyler, good morning, it's Connie."

He quickly responded, "Connie, last night was great! Thank you so much for everything."

I told Skyler that I had a dream from God and wanted to share it with him. He anxiously said, "Yes, please do."

"In the dream, you appeared to have three snake bites on the side of your neck. After the third snake bite had taken place, you were totally healed of this cancer."

Skyler screamed with joy. "Connie, I have always described my chemo as poison. So yes, the three bites are the chemo treatments. But what you don't know is that my body can only receive three more chemo treatments and afterward—none whatsoever."

As we cried together, we knew that he was going to get his sought-after miracle healing—and not long from now.

Shortly after this amazing experience, my husband's work schedule changed, and we could no longer continue the weekly Bible study.

It was actually better, as we had another package of joy coming our way soon—our second son, Stephen!

Five years later, we were invited to a Bat mitzvah. I booked a babysitter and prepared for the evening out.

Walking into the hotel event, we viewed a large crowd, beautifully dressed. Chandeliers clustered above us, while ahead of us, a sea of ivory tablecloths—laced with crystal goblets and pristine china. The ice sculpture was encircled with chocolate-covered strawberries, and a spacious canopy embraced a plethora of cream-colored roses.

We spotted some friends and walked over to say hello. As we were greeting them, I heard a familiar voice practically shout my name. It was a woman who attended our Bible study five years before. She shouted once again and said:

"Connie, did you see Skyler?"

I answered, "What? Skyler is here? Where?"

My friend pointed in the direction where Skyler was. He stood tall in his perfectly tailored suit. Instead of a hat, a full head of hair graced him. He smiled endlessly at his friends. As I approached him, I wondered if he'd remember me.

After polar bear hugs, Skyler shared that he graduated from law school and had an intern job in a successful attorney's office downtown. He told me the cancer had left him immediately after the three chemo treatments, and had never returned.

Not only did Skyler remember me, but he remembered every detail of that life-changing night, long ago.

"God, thank You for healing dear Skyler. You took a young man's great measure of faith and brought forth a miracle. To You, God, belongs all the glory. You are worthy to be praised!"

CHAPTER TEN

The Phone Call

Do we put restrictions on God's supernatural power? Have we established boundaries, closing Him off from performing miracles in our lives?

By limiting God's flow of His divine acts, we could miss out on the exciting events that He would perform.

When my son, Joshua, was six months old, I signed him up for swimming classes at the YMCA. *There's an ambitious mother for you!*

The day for our first lesson came. We made our way, like two amateur ice skaters on the slippery, bleach-soaked tiles to the pool.

In the water stood a couple twirling their white-blond-haired baby girl, in hope of preventing her from crying. The father of this giggling, chlorine-drenched child looked familiar. It wasn't until he introduced himself that I realized we had met a long time ago in acting class. It was great to see him again. Nate, his wife, Cathy, and their baby, Katie, were a beautiful family.

A couple of years later, as we enrolled Joshua into Sunny Preschool, our paths crossed again. Cathy was enrolling Katie. While reconnecting, it became apparent that we lived close together, so made carpool arrangements.

Cathy stood five feet nine inches in her thin frame. Long, blond hair staged her narrow face nicely, as she bent down to buckle up her child and shout out a big, fat "hello!"

Before long, we filled our cars with four preschool students. I had enrolled my second son, Stephen, and Cathy—her second daughter, Carry.

Spring break came and went, and Sunny Preschool would, once again, open its friendly doors. I called Cathy to plan our carpool schedule. She didn't answer, so I left a message.

After a few days had passed, I started wondering why I hadn't heard back from her.

One evening, my husband and I were reading in bed when the phone rang at 8:30 PM. My husband answered to hear Cathy's cheerful, trumpeting voice. He handed the phone to me and listened along to the captivating conversation.

Cathy sang out, "Hi Connie, this is Cathy."

"Oh, hi Cathy, did you get my message?"

Her reply shockingly surprised both my husband and me.

She said, "I'm not at home. I'm at the hospital. I have a 107-degree temperature—and they don't know what's wrong with me. They say I'm dying. Well, I better go now. Bye."

Without taking a breath, I shouted, "Wait! Don't hang up. Cathy, are you there?"

"Yes, I'm here," she softly answered.

Being concerned that Cathy would hang up, I knew that I had to act quickly. I asked, "What do you mean, you're dying?"

With no emotion whatsoever, as though Cathy was telling me about the weather, she proclaimed: "Oh, as I said, they don't know what's wrong with me—just that I'm dying. Well, I better go now."

Once again, with a high level of adrenalin kicking-in, I shouted, "Cathy, please don't hang up! I have to pray for you."

With a passive voice, she replied, "Okay."

Taking the initiative to pray, I did so, loudly. While pleading with God to save Cathy's life, I rebuked Satan and death from her. I cried out for a complete healing and an accurate diagnosis as soon as possible. I prayed that her temperature would go to normal, immediately.

As I neared the end of my prayer, barely finishing with the words, "In Jesus' name," Cathy cheerfully said goodbye.

I hung up the phone and looked at my husband, who asked, "Is there some reasonable explanation for what I just heard?"

It occurred to me to call Cathy's husband, but I didn't know where Cathy was calling from and assumed Nate was there by her side.

My pillowcase wet with tears, and my mind racing through tunnels of sleeplessness—I waited for the birds to sing outside my window, as the first glimpse of morning showed through.

It was early when the phone rang. I awkwardly grasped it to hear the voice of Cathy's husband. "Connie, it's Nate. I know you called about carpool last week, but Cathy couldn't get back to you." After a large pause, he said, "How do I start to tell you about this unbelievable miracle?"

As I carefully listened, I could tell that Nate had no idea I had spoken to and prayed for Cathy the night before. I clung to his word, *"miracle."*

Not wanting to be in suspense a moment longer, I asked, "How's Cathy?"

"Connie, Cathy almost died last night. As a matter of fact, the doctor told me to say my last goodbye and to go home to my girls—that she wouldn't make it through the night. So I left the hospital about 7:30 PM and went home. This morning upon awakening, I wondered why I hadn't heard anything from the doctor or the hospital. I hoped it was a good sign—that perhaps Cathy *did* make it through the night. When I got to the hospital this morning and walked into her room, I couldn't believe my eyes! There was Cathy, sitting up in bed laughing with the nurses, as I watched in unbelief. She told me that her fever broke last night, but they were closely observing her—still not knowing what was wrong."

I couldn't take it any longer, so asked, "Nate, did Cathy tell you about our phone conversation last night?"

He responded in a heartbeat. "What? There is no way Cathy could have spoken to you or *anyone* last night. When did you call?"

I responded even more quickly, "No, Nate. I didn't call her—she called *me* at 8:30 PM."

"Connie," he insisted, "Believe me, you must've been dreaming. Cathy couldn't talk. When I left here last night at 7:30 PM, she was in a coma and on morphine. She was also nowhere near the phone, which by the way, is across the room from her bed. Besides, the doctor said she was dying and wouldn't make it through the night."

Bewildered, I then asked Nate to ask Cathy if she remembered calling me. She didn't. In fact, she told him that she didn't remember anything about the night, didn't have her address book with her, and didn't have my phone number memorized.

I boldly told Nate, once again, that Cathy indeed called me last night. To convince him of this truth, I handed the phone to my husband. He told Nate that he had heard the entire conversation, and that it was *he* who initially answered the phone.

There was silence. I wondered what I should do. I broke the silence with an invitation for Nate to come to our home and pray with us for Cathy. Shortly thereafter, he arrived, and we immediately started to pray.

Even though Cathy's temperature was under control, we prayed that the doctors would bring an infectious disease specialist in—who would be able to diagnose this mysterious illness.

Nate began to question me about my faith, in which I promptly answered with joy. Afterward, he told me that he wanted *my* faith and asked how to get it.

Soon, I was leading Nate in a prayer to receive Jesus Christ as his Lord and Savior. In my living room, Nate was *born again*. I gave him a Bible, and he was on his way back to the hospital.

Later that night, Nate called with astonishing news. An infectious disease specialist flew in from New York to diagnose Cathy, and found she had

Legionnaires' disease. There was only one antibiotic that could possibly cure it. They started her on the medicine immediately.

I prayed with Nate that Cathy would have a full and speedy recovery. God, once again, heard our petitions. Cathy was released from the hospital the next day with orders for bed rest. One week later, we were carpooling as if nothing had ever happened.

The school year was rapidly coming to a close. I wondered if we would remain friends with Cathy and her family since the children were moving on to separate schools. Would the bond that we made during Cathy's dramatic healing hold?

Soon into the summer, I had a vivid dream about Cathy and saw that she was pregnant with her third child. I called her right away to share the dream. She sternly assured me that they were not planning for another child.

Time escaped us, as summer quickly raced ahead to meet with fall. It had been a couple of years since my sons had attended Sunny Preschool, and were nicely adjusted in their new location. Homework, sports, and multiple activities kept them very busy.

One late afternoon, I was jogging, as Stephen was practicing with his soccer team on the grassy area that centered the track. On my third time around the field, I heard a familiar, cheerful voice shout out to me: "Connie!"

It was Cathy!

She pointed toward a group of girls gathered around on the grass. There, in the midst of them, sat a small little girl with white-blond hair.

Cathy declared, "There, Connie, is your dream!"

As we conversed, Cathy reminded me that she and Nate were not going to have another child, but expressed that this surprise was a true blessing.

I held my sweet son's hand on the way home in the car. "Always believe in miracles," I told him.

I kissed my two sons goodnight and slept on my tear-dampened pillow. I knew that *these* tears were tears of joy.

It wasn't Cathy's time to die. She had a calling to be a mother of—not two—but three girls. God, in His outrageously uncommon ways, used *one phone call* to put a miracle in motion!

CHAPTER ELEVEN

There, Around the Corner

When God speaks to us and gives us direction, it may be in general or in great detail. This time, the details were *very* clear and precise.

Every day, I am committed to set aside time to read the Word of God and pray. One sunny morning, I was reading in my bedroom on the comfortable chaise—giving my feet a good rest. A window view revealed soft, pink azaleas which seemed to be looking back at me, as if to say, "Good morning."

Often, I seek God to show me what good I could do in the present day. This particular morning, He answered me with sharply defined direction. As I became silent before Him, I heard these words:

"When you take your morning walk, around the corner you will see a woman with very dark hair walking up the hill toward you. Mary will politely introduce herself to you and ask you a question about the Holy Spirit."

I couldn't wait to get going and see this unusual event come to pass. After finishing my prayers, I quickly readied myself for my walk and to meet this woman with very dark hair named, Mary.

Starting out from my house, I felt led to go right, then down the hill on Austin Street.

There she was! A woman with very dark hair, walking up the hill toward me. God had said that she would politely stop *me*, so I was trying to avoid any eye contact between us. Knowing that this was God's plan, not mine, I didn't want to manipulate the situation. While focused on the sidewalk, I heard a soft, sweet voice:

"Excuse me. I certainly don't want to bother you on your morning walk, but may I just ask you a question?"

In a whirlwind of anticipation, I answered, "Of course!"

"My name is *Mary*. I live down the hill about two blocks over." Mary paused, and then said, "I want to ask you a question about the Holy Spirit."

"Absolutely," I sounded. Excitement exploded within, while witnessing God's great power—the way that He arranged this meeting so supernaturally.

I looked deep into Mary's searching brown eyes and said, "I would be happier than you can imagine, to answer any question you have."

Hand in hand, we walked for nearly an hour, as I happily answered the question she had about the Holy Spirit.

Several years had gone by. I had no idea that it would be so long before I would see Mary again.

One day, I saw her walking with a dog. "Mary," I called out, "It's been so long! How have you been?"

Mary and I took another walk, as she shared the past years of grief. Her husband had become very ill and she needed to nurse him full time until he passed. This was one of the first walks she had taken since we first met.

Mary expressed how she could not have endured those years of hardship if it had not been for the help of the Holy Spirit.

> *"Lord, thank You for helping this dear woman through such trying years. I ask that You please continue to use me to speak hope into lives like Mary's. Keep me ready!"*

CHAPTER TWELVE

The Visit

You never know when you may have a surprise visit from someone very special. This visitor came at a unique time for all of us. But most importantly, for my son, Stephen—a vision of hope.

It was the end of December, when our family started to reflect on the past year while anticipating the next to come. We sat around the kitchen table, taking turns sharing our thoughts.

Stephen, our enthusiastic and clever three-year-old, sat focused, as he maneuvered his small, metal car across the wooden table. His white-blond hair was enhanced by the kitchen light above him, which also lightened the crystal blue of his eyes.

Joshua, our vibrant five-year-old, was quite an opposite image from Stephen. His shiny brown hair and olive skin complemented his eyes of chocolate. He shared his plans and goals for the next year—as we warmly attended to his dreams.

Lauren, who had just turned twelve, was anxious to play a family game. She sat at the end of the table in a welcoming window seat. Her sky-blue eyes sparkled, as we moved our attention to her.

She shyly spoke, "I'm so happy to have a family like this." We were all in one accord.

Our special evening included routine, bedtime story-reading which was enjoyed by all of us. After bubbly baths and squeaky-clean cheeks, all lights were out, and the children were in their cozy beds. Lauren was in her room downstairs, and the boys were in their bedrooms adjacent to ours.

That night, I had a dream from God that was prophetic—and years later, came to pass. I felt the Lord's presence in our home and was joyously soaking it up.

I was awakened early, at around 6:00 AM, when I heard Stephen calling me to come into his room.

Upon entering, I knew something was different. The room was filled with God's glory and appeared to embrace a luminous atmosphere. Stephen was sitting up in his small-framed bed, and called me over to his side. His eyes, seeming more blue and lighter than ever, stared into mine—as he excitedly stated:

"Mommy, Jesus was here!"

I had no doubt what Stephen said was true. But wanting to hear every detail, I asked, "Jesus was right here in your room?"

"Yes," he said, with total confidence. "He was here, and He left."

"Stephen, what did He look like?"

My young son replied as if I should have already known what Jesus looks like. "You know—like Jesus, Mommy!"

I sat down next to Stephen, clinging to every word that he said, and asked, "What was He wearing?"

"A long robe with gold bells all around on the bottom with things like apples. There was a bell, then an apple, then a bell." Stephen described it so precisely.

Continuing, Stephen's countenance brightened when he spoke about Jesus. I knew he had seen Him.

"Mom, I woke up and saw Jesus coming down into my room. There were a lot of big angels lowering him down through the ceiling. Then, He stood next to a door."

Excitedly, I asked, "What did the door look like?"

"Mommy, it's not *the* door, it's *His* door," he exclaimed.

"Stephen, what did Jesus say to you?"

"He said for me to come through His door. So I did, Mommy. It was so beautiful! He took me, and we flew around. I saw so many things. I saw Heaven. It was like a city. It was so beautiful! But, He then took me to a bad place, and had me look down a drain. I saw ugly, scary men down there, and it was so dark!"

With a gasp in my breath, I asked, "What happened then, Stephen?"

"We came back to my room, and the angels lifted Jesus up through my ceiling—and they were gone. I wish He could have stayed. I really wanted Him to!"

Time escaped me, and I knew I needed to wake everyone up to get ready for church. I popped my head into Joshua's room, as he awoke promptly to tell me about his dream of Heaven, and clearly stated of its beauty.

My emotions were in a flurry, as I ran down the stairs to awake Lauren. It always took this pre-teen many nudges and gentle shakes to wake up. She loved sleeping in, and looked forward to every opportunity to do so. As I opened the door of her room, I was shocked to see her spring up so quickly with eyes ablaze, as she spoke these words:

"Mom, I had the most remarkable dream—or was it a vision? I'm not sure, but it was real! I was sitting in Joshua's room upstairs with Daddy, and I looked out the window and saw a door up in

Heaven. The door opened, and a stream of light came down to our house. Then, I heard the sound of music, like beautiful bells. I waited for Jesus to come and see me, but He never came. Mom, why didn't He come to see me?"

I looked at Lauren, and proclaimed, "Because, He went to see Stephen."

Taking Lauren's hand in mine, I said, "Sweetheart, the Lord did indeed visit all of us last night in different ways. For some reason, He spent more time with Stephen."

We stayed home that night and celebrated New Year's Eve together, basking in the glory of God that still remained. We repeatedly shared our own experiences from the night before, as we looked up the description of the robe that Stephen had said Jesus was wearing.

The Bible describes the High Priest robe as the one Stephen saw. It had gold bells alternating with pomegranates on the hem of the robe. Those *pomegranates* were Stephen's *apples*.

My family and I will never forget that majestic night. I believe that the Lord Jesus is far more reachable than we can imagine. Who knows when and where He may visit again?

CHAPTER THIRTEEN

The Great Escape

While waiting at my neighbor's, I watched out their window, as workmen raced frantically to save our home.

God's grace is sufficient, I thought, as I tried to stay calm. Little could I have dreamed what morning would bring. *God, You have never failed me.*

Pulling the straps up over my heels, I grabbed my purse and coat, ran to the car, and jumped in.

"Okay, everyone, do we have everything? Joshua and Stephen, do you have your robes?"

"Yes, mommy," they replied, like two angels in the back seat.

This was *Christmas Carol Night*. Our family anticipated it with joy every year. Joshua was now in first grade and Stephen in pre-kindergarten.

What a tradition this event held for over sixty-five years. It was a blessing to be a part of this historic family—*The John Thomas Dye School.*

We parked nearby and ran quickly through the downpour of rain. The street had become a stream of rapid-rolling waves, where my feet became immersed in a deluge of rainwater. *Should have worn my boots!*

Approaching Dye Hall, we delighted in the sweet aroma of homemade gingerbread. An oversized, silver punch bowl centered the long mahogany table, while tempting the guests to partake of hot apple cider.

Tradition! Yes, and we loved it. The Hall was decked with fresh pine wreaths displaying simple, yet elegant, decor. Garland was draped from one post to the next which made its way around the rafters.

The parents proudly viewed their children in white choir robes, as they prepared to sing Christmas and Hanukah songs. Once we spotted the locations of our children, we relaxed and watched the show. Pride enveloped me, as I heard my precious sons sing with zeal.

When the performance was over, we weathered the storm on our way back to our home. My children were warm in their beds by eight o'clock. I wanted to get into bed early as well, since we were leaving soon for our traditional Hawaiian trip during Christmas break.

My husband, Peter, quietly came up the stairs without my noticing, as he tried not to wake me. But I did awake at two o'clock in the morning.

I stood out of bed and proclaimed: "Our house is in danger. Our house is in danger. It's filling up. It's filling up."

I remember slipping back into bed with no understanding of what I had just said. Peter, though, remembered all the times I had spoken a warning from God—and decided to take precautionary action. He thought that perhaps the house could be flooding with rain, so ventured downstairs to find the unexpected.

Suddenly, I was awakened as Peter shook me. His dark-brown eyes screamed with alarm, as he shouted:

"Connie, our house is filling up with gas! Get the children. We have to leave immediately!"

As Peter ran outside to try and turn off our gas, I calmly went into our children's rooms. "Sons, get your robes and slippers on, grab your pillows and teddy bears, and meet me in my room."

Within seconds, they were standing at attention in my room to receive more direction. Seemingly, neither of them panicked nor worried. It was as though we were playing-out parts in a movie, and somehow knew the ending would be safe.

With little knowledge of gas leaks, I did everything wrong. I turned on and off light switches, opened the garage door—and to my disbelief—started the car.

In a moment of time, we were parked in the driveway awaiting Peter. I had already called the gas company, who in turn, was arranging to send help.

Looking out of the car window, I saw panic on Peter's face, as he raced toward us.

"Get away from the house, I can't stop the gas!"

I responded with concern, "Do you have the right wrench?"

Our conversation came to a halt when we saw two large gas company trucks pull up to our home. Two smaller trucks followed. The men jumped out of the vehicles and quickly ran into our house through the front door, and just as quickly, ran out again. One man then shouted out to us:

"My meter can't tell me how much gas is in your house—it only goes up so far. Please get away! Go to your neighbors. Your house could explode into flames at any time."

I was filled with a barrage of dreaded fear. *Our home—where I brought my babies up. Our photos—that we can never replace.*

Then, I heard the sweet voice of my six-year-old son, Joshua. "Mama, don't go back into the house, it isn't worth it. We have all we need. We have each other." Stephen then agreed, heartily.

We spent the night across the street at our neighbor's home. I settled my sons into the spare bedroom, and positioned myself near the window, where I watched the great feat.

We don't realize what we have until it starts slipping away from us. It wasn't only the material aspect of our home, but the memories it beheld that I treasured.

At five o'clock in the morning, I saw one of the workmen coming in our direction. I heard loud knocking on our neighbor's door and ran as quickly as I could, while avoiding stumbling in the dark.

"You and your family can come back to your home if you stay upstairs all day with the windows opened."

Elated with the news, I gathered my precious sons and their belongings. The moment we entered our home, I rushed the boys up the stairs to my room that had plenty of large windows to open. I tucked them into my bed, and ran downstairs to speak to the workmen. The large trucks had gone, but at my door, stood one of the men to tell me what had happened.

"Ma'am, you are very lucky! If you and your family had stayed in your beds for ten minutes longer, all of you would have died in your sleep. The main gas pipe, which feeds your home and several other surrounding homes, had cracked."

He started motioning with his hands and continued: "The gas was forced to move into the outer pipe, which surrounds your service pipe, and travel into your home at a steady speed. So no matter how hard your husband tried to turn off the gas, it wouldn't have worked. We turned off the main flow to all of your homes and replaced the broken main. And now your service is back on. Your neighbors are truly lucky as well. The gas was already in the pipes traveling to their homes. Eventually, your house would have exploded—then the chain reaction would have begun."

As I grasped this kind man's words, I thanked him for his hard work throughout the night. But I couldn't let him go until I told him of how God awakened me at two o'clock in the morning to warn us of trouble. I shared how God had protected us and our neighbors and also used him and his crew to come to our rescue—and that I was forever grateful.

The man shook my hand then walked away toward his small truck. I'm sure he had a lot to think about, as we all did.

Only a few days later, we were sitting on the beach in Hawaii. I couldn't help but think, time-and-time-again, how blessed we were to be there. If God had not intervened in our lives, we would have all died that rainy night. But we have an awesome God, who is our protector and rescuer in time of trouble.

Perhaps we had more things to accomplish, or perhaps it just wasn't our time.

As I watched my sons play in the sand, I looked up to Heaven and said, *"Lord, You are faithful. Thank You with all that I am."*

CHAPTER FOURTEEN

Faith Heals

How was I to stay calm when my child was in extreme pain?

Was it possible to prevent something from happening when I knew it was coming? Could I have done anything differently to change the outcome? I asked myself these questions when the accident occurred.

One evening, while helping my son, Stephen, brush his teeth, God presented a picture—or more like a home video right before my eyes.

I viewed my other son, Joshua, on the upper part of the bunk bed in Stephen's room. I saw him fall onto the floor and grab his left wrist, while crying out in pain.

After the vision stopped, I yelled out, "Joshua, are you on top of Stephen's bunk bed?"

"Yes, mommy. I'm being careful. I won't fall."

That night, the boys slept well.

The very next night, I once again studied Stephen's attempt to have whiter, brighter teeth.

The sound of a sudden thump jolted me, as I quickly ran into Stephen's room. Joshua was on the floor grabbing his left wrist and crying with excruciating pain: "Mommy, help me!"

I couldn't believe it! The vision from the night before had happened. *Why didn't God prevent this accident? He knew it was coming. Did I pray after God had shown me this? Could I have stopped it?*

One thing the vision did do, was prepare me so that I was able to remain calm. It was agonizing, though, to see my sweet Joshua in that much pain. But my faith carried me through it.

The next morning, we went to Dr. Kevin Bear's office. We knew Kevin well, as we were neighbors and friends. He was a gentle man with a great reputation in the medical field. We affectionately called him, Dr. K.

X-rays were taken, which proved that Joshua indeed, broke his wrist. After the examination, the nurse took Joshua into another room to be fitted for a cast. I confronted Dr. K:

"Joshua will need a removable cast since we will be going on vacation in a little over a week. He'll be swimming and playing in the sand."

Dr. K's response made me laugh.

"You really do expect a lot, don't you? Joshua will need to wear a cast for at least a month."

He booked us to come back in before our trip. I reminded him to have the removable cast ready for my son.

During that long week, leading up to the appointment, my family and I continued to pray for a speedy recovery for Joshua.

We returned to see Dr. K, and after the x-ray was taken, it showed that Joshua's wrist was almost completely healed—which meant that he could have a removable cast.

Dr. K was truly shocked and very happy for Joshua. He kept commenting on how amazing this was, and that Joshua's shortened recovery was quite a miracle.

> *God not only works things together for good in our own lives, but touches others in the process. He is worthy to be praised!*

CHAPTER FIFTEEN

Valentine's Day

Valentine's Day had never been one of my favorite holidays or celebrations. As you read this story, though, you will see how and why I changed my mind.

The doorbell rang, and I quickly ran to greet Abby. Dressed in a crimson-red blouse and peasant skirt, her hair perfectly blown—she smiled shyly, and apologized for being early.

Our weekly Bible study started at 11:00 AM. It was 10:45 AM, so Abby wasn't *that* early.

Abby had been waiting for a kidney. She had a deadline for the transplant, and was getting anxious because time was running out.

As we walked together to the *green-room,* she started to tell me of the urgent status.

"They haven't found a match for me, so I have to rush off from our meeting this morning to get to my doctor's office." Awaiting her would be a home-kit to prepare for the dreaded dialysis.

Abby warned me that she didn't want prayer. She felt bitter toward God for not hearing and answering our desperate requests for her.

I offered affection, but she seemed closed to it. So I backed off carefully, respecting her mood.

We sat silently waiting for the others to arrive. It was awkward and I found myself straightening everything in the room. She looked steadily out the window at the sprawling clouds. My heart was getting heavy watching her.

Finally, the others arrived and we were soon beginning our meeting. I've held on to a tradition of praise reports, Bible teaching, singing, and prayer. It seemed to always work nicely, but *this* morning held a heaviness that was not common to us.

After praise reports, Abby explained to the group of her emergent situation. Everyone held back tears, as we started to pray. I closed my eyes and silently pleaded with the Lord to bring forth a miracle for my friend. Then, unexpectedly, the Lord said to me:

"Abby will not need to have dialysis."

I sat quietly, hoping there was more, but that was all I heard. I knew without a doubt that I had heard God's voice. I moved my way over to where Abby was sitting. I knelt next to her and said, "Abby, you will not need to have dialysis!"

Quickly, a redness developed under Abby's transparent skin as she glared at me to say, "I told you what is happening, and now you say this?"

I replied, "I know it's hard to believe, but God has it all under control. Whatever His plan is, it will somehow prove that you won't need dialysis."

She spoke no longer, and left immediately after the prayers. I watched her dash out the front door and wondered what God had in mind for this dear, hurting woman.

Later that afternoon, my sons were enjoying after-school snacks when I answered the phone. It was Mindy, a close friend of Abby's. She exuberantly proclaimed: "Connie, you won't believe this! Abby walked into the doctor's office to receive her pre-dialysis kit and the nurse told her that she didn't need one now. They have a donor for her!"

"What a mighty God we serve, and a last-minute one," I answered.

After we hung up, I knelt down in the green-room, where we had prayed that morning, to thank and praise God.

I later learned that the donor had been a college roommate of Abby's. Upon hearing of Abby's needs, Johanna secretly got tested to see if she was a match. She had enough components to donate her kidney to her old friend.

Before long, they were in surgery together, side-by-side. The transition was a great success, ending in celebration. I could just imagine the reunion these two experienced, as they traveled step-by-step through this healing process.

Abby's body didn't try to reject its new member—and her beloved friend healed perfectly.

Now, each Valentine's Day that passes brings a special memory. Instead of chocolates and red hearts, my own heart melts with love and admiration for our Creator!

CHAPTER SIXTEEN

Unfinished Business

If you believe that God can perform the seemingly impossible at any time He chooses, then you will love this story. If you aren't sure that He can, then this story may change your life.

God is the same that He was two thousand years ago. His mercies endure forever. He will bring healing and life to those who hunger for, and believe in His majesty.

I'd heard of how important forgiveness was in God's eyes, but could have never imagined He would go this far to bring it to a family!

It was a still, gray afternoon which brought about a craving for my beloved breakfast tea. Once it was ready, I nestled into my cushy chair accompanied with an ottoman. While my sons were in school, I wanted to use the valued time to read my Bible and pray.

No more than a minute into my journaling, I heard the Lord speak to me. A gentle, loving voice brought forth these words:

"Connie, I want you to start a weekly prayer meeting and Bible study for women—here in your home."

Although, I was excited to start a group, I asked God to confirm this to me through two or more believers.

The confirmations came quickly during the week from two women I respected. The only thing that seemed crystal clear at the time, was that this group would be opened to women attending various Christian denominations and non-denominations.

During that same week there was an event at the preschool both my sons were attending. I always loved visiting the old, country-style house and the large, inviting backyard.

The directress of the school was a very animated and energetic lady. Ms. Rhonda's hair was a subtle-bronze with blond highlights. Her eyes glowed a light, meadow-green.

Her bright smile appeared, as she approached me to discuss my son's advanced work with puzzles. She commented that he was quite methodical and articulate.

During our conversation, she asked me whether I knew of any women's Bible studies nearby. I started to answer, but was kindly interrupted by her suggesting I start one at my home. *Well,* I thought, *isn't this coincidental.*

Two weeks later, three women came to attend the first weekly meeting. One of these women became a close friend for many years to come. Sandy stood around five feet eight inches tall, and had curly, jet-black hair that tousled every time she laughed.

Sandy admitted to being extremely depressed that first meeting. I knew hard work was before me at the onset of this ministry, and asked for God's guidance and wisdom. She shared that her husband, Eric, was a longtime diabetic who had the unfortunate loss of one leg. Sandy had been nursing her husband for several years which eventually produced an onslaught of problems in their marriage. This included the loss of their home caused by a huge amount of medical bills.

Sandy cried endlessly, as we did everything we could to comfort her and give her hope. My heart was crushed for this hurting woman. I pondered and searched for a way in which I could contribute to her needs.

It then occurred to me that I could hire her to housesit for us while we were away. At first, I approached the idea as a favor—not wanting to touch the very sensitive areas of her life.

She responded with joy and was back at our home that week. She diligently watched over the property and cared for our dogs, while we attended an event out of town.

On our return, it was clear that our pets liked Sandy and, of course, we paid her generously for her time.

Sandy became a part of our family. One day she told me she'd like for me to meet her husband. I agreed and we made a date.

On my way to their home for lunch, I prayed that the Lord would give me the appropriate words to minister to Eric.

Handing my hosts a gift of chocolate covered almonds, I walked into their spacious apartment. It was large for just two people and had a nice flow for entertaining.

A table in the center of the dining room, colorfully decorated with scrumptious food, caught my attention. My Middle-Eastern favorites awaited me, including; boiled eggs with homemade hummus, greens drizzled with olive oil, and freshly baked pita bread with wild honey. It all reminded me of a delicious meal that was prepared by a friend while we visited Israel, years ago. Sandy and Eric's hospitality both impressed and humbled me.

After we ate, our conversation turned toward the Lord and His grace. In little time, I had the enormous blessing of leading Eric in a prayer to accept Jesus as his Lord and Savior. It was a heavenly afternoon, and the best part was the last.

Over a course of a few months, we became more concerned for Eric. His health was greatly declining and there was talk of another amputation, which would leave dear Eric without legs.

That horrifying thought came into play just a few weeks later. Upon hearing the news, I began to plead with God to intervene and help this family.

During my supplications, a sensation of peace found its way into my weary heart. I knew that I needed to rely on the reality that God *knows* all things and can *do* all things.

After the surgery and a speedy recovery for Eric, they moved into a smaller apartment. There, it would be more conducive for Sandy to keep up while spending most of her time nurturing her husband.

A few months later, in the early hours of the morning, I awoke with anticipation that the Lord was going to speak to me.

While sitting on the side of my bed, I heard the Lord's voice say:

"I am taking Eric home today."

I waited until 8:30 AM to make my call to Sandy, hoping not to wake anyone. Sandy answered the phone with an indescribable, pained voice.

Through her sobs, she explained that Eric had been going in and out of consciousness and saying, "Look, see the little angel at the foot of my bed?"

I assured Sandy that I would come over once I did my morning errands. My boys were in school and I knew I could be there to help Sandy and Eric. But my timing is not always in sync with God's.

Finishing my morning rituals, I was off to the market. While approaching an intersection, the Lord spoke to me quite clearly:

"Go there now!"

In a flash, I made a quick left turn and was on my way to Sandy and Eric's apartment.

It does amaze me how we so often get tangled in our own routines in life, while putting the more important matters on hold. I knew I had a work to do that day for God and I was trying to do it in my own timing—in my own way.

While parking in front of the apartment, I prayed that God would give me wisdom on how to minister to this family. God had told me upon awakening that He was taking Eric home this day. But did the family know that, as well?

Upon entering their home, I sensed that death was at hand. Sandy seemed drained of her natural color and their daughter appeared to be in a daze. Their son and his fiancée were timid.

We entered the bedroom, which was medium sized with foam-green walls which exaggerated the white bedding neatly tucked around Eric.

As gracefully as I could, I asked the family to sit on the bed and circle around Eric. As they found their places, I placed my fingers against Eric's wrist to check his pulse. I had learned in a CPR class how to do this. Eric had not been officially declared dead, but I felt no pulse, whatsoever. I then pressed my fingers into the side of his neck. Nothing!

The Holy Spirit led me through the next remarkable twenty minutes. I explained of the great importance to God that family members forgive one another before one "goes home." They listened to my words, while eager to execute whatever needed to be done, in order to make things right. They quickly agreed with me to hold hands, then looked to me for the next move. The Lord then spoke these life changing words to me:

> *"Bring Eric back, and have him say, 'I forgive you and love you,' to each one. Then have each one say the same back to Eric.' "*

I informed the family that I was going to wake Eric up, to enable him to forgive each one—and each one, to forgive him.

They all stared at me with anticipation, as I started to speak to their beloved.

"Eric, you must wake up now. Come back, in Jesus' name!"

Immediately, Eric's eyes opened. He was very alert, while I explained what we were going to do and say. Eric smiled, and began to speak the words to one member of his family at a time, around the circle—as they, one-by-one, responded back to him. With deepest sincerity, the family made peace with one another.

Once the proclamations were finished, Eric pointed to the foot of the bed. With a welcoming smile, he exclaimed, "Look, see—there's the angel again!"

Those words became the last words that Eric spoke. He closed his eyes and became unconscious.

Feeling very peaceful, I hugged the family and was on my way to continue my day. I put my praise music on in the car and relaxed. I purchased items to bring Sandy and her family later for their dinner. But on my way home from the market, once again, God spoke, *"Go back there now!"*

I decided not to be foolish, but to obey God's voice. I quickly made a turn and was on my way back to their apartment, accompanied with ice cream in the trunk.

As I turned the corner onto their street, in full view was a paramedic's truck. I parked my car, and ran up the stairs to their apartment, thinking they'd be speedier than the elevator.

Upon entering the apartment, there were three paramedics working relentlessly to save poor Eric's life. The image was almost too much for me. This frail, shortened body being tossed about by sincere workers, trying to save him.

A voice filled with hysteria, coming from the kitchen, distracted me. I found Sandy, barely keeping herself upright on the edge of a large chopping block in the center of the room. She was holding a handkerchief over her red, swollen face.

I lovingly whispered in her ear, "Sandy, let's let go. Let's let Eric go."

She yelled out, "I don't want him to die! Please God, don't let him die!"

Echoing once again in my heart were the words the Lord gave me that very morning, telling me that He was taking Eric home this day.

I gently grabbed Sandy's upper arms so she'd look into my eyes. With compassion, and yet boldness, I said, "Sandy, I know that it is hard to let someone go that you love so much. But you don't want Eric to suffer any longer. If you let him go, I believe God will take him right now."

With that, she became more hysterical, so I led her into the hallway to see Eric on the floor. Her emotions calmed, as she stared down at him. A peace came upon her as she turned to me saying, "Yes, Connie. I will let him go into the arms of Jesus. Lord, please take Eric home now."

I helped Sandy sit securely in a chair back in the kitchen, as I stretched my neck to see down the hall.

I saw Eric's motionless body. The Lord took him home, as dear Sandy was able to let him go.

Very peacefully, Sandy said:

"He's gone."

She gracefully walked over to where they had laid Eric on the gurney and pressed the back of her hand gently across his forehead and down his cheek and whispered:

"Oh Eric, I love you dear."

As I observed Sandy's loving touches, I knew that she had sincerely let him go. She turned once again to me and said, "He's with Jesus. All is well."

Once Sandy and I were alone at the end of the day, she looked at me with damp eyes and said, "That was a miracle earlier this morning, wasn't it Connie?"

I said, "Yes, Sandy, a miracle indeed!"

That night, I slept peacefully, believing that Sandy did too. Reflecting on the day, I prayed:

"Thank You Lord, that You brought deeply needed forgiveness and peace to this family before Eric died. Thank You for your mercy. You are beyond marvelous!"

CHAPTER SEVENTEEN

The Secret behind 'Saved by the Bell'

In memory of the late Brandon Tartikoff

Who *really* came up with the idea of a television show for kids and teens that is still playing today? How did this all come about in a divine way?

It was the mid-eighties, and our sons, Joshua and Stephen, were the joy of our lives. We treasured every moment with them.

My husband and I had rules, and set up boundaries for our children's lives—one concerning television viewing. They could watch TV only at limited intervals. Reading and learning about the world—its history and arts—always came first.

On Saturday mornings, we gave our sons a window of time to watch TV. It was a nice break between all of their commitments. But there was nothing that we deemed wholesome or educational for them to watch. Cartoons monopolized the screen—not our first choice for our children.

Peter's career as a television producer brought many challenges. He had been struggling with the choices of material and subject matter that was being offered to him. We started to seek God for clarity in his next move.

After much discussion and prayer, we both agreed that it would be great for him to work on something that children and teens could watch. Something entertaining, funny, and would include a good moral to be learned.

Our prayer was soon answered through a dream.

After a long day of carpooling my sons to different extra-curricular programs, I settled into my bed. After reading some Scriptures and prayer, I slipped into a sweet sleep. I awoke early in the morning with great excitement about the dream that God had given me:

Peter and I were in Covina, walking along on a sidewalk outside of the elementary school I attended as a child. I took notice that Peter was wearing a suit and tie. We crossed the street over to the school's property and entered the administration building.

We were asked to wait in a classroom before seeing the principal of the school. We sat for a short while, then were asked in to see him.

> *We spent a brief time in his office until he escorted us to a high school where he had us sit in a classroom full of teens. We stayed in that classroom for a very long time.*

After sharing the dream with Peter, I explained the interpretation of it:

> *"We are going to do a show for children based on the experiences in the classroom at an elementary school. Then, not long afterward, we move it to high school with teens. This show will go on-and-on for many years—and you, Peter, will be the executive producer."*

Peter said, "Okay!"

I was excited that God was orchestrating our future and Peter's career. We both felt hopeful that we would be making a television show for children. After all, that was our specific prayer.

I'm sure that our faith was being tested during the wait. We knew that we had a show to do—but when would it begin?

After a season of prayer, Peter was offered a contract from NBC to develop television shows. He quickly moved into an office in Burbank. Peter was excited to be working with Brandon Tartikoff, who was the president of entertainment. We believed that this was the link to the show for children.

Peter stretched himself to work hard at coming up with some ideas. We both remembered the dream that God had given us.

But how to begin?

One day, we were both invited to a breakfast related to our church activities. Since the meeting would be held in the Valley, we took two cars, parked them in the lot at NBC, and rode together.

Once the event was over, we were on our way back to my car. I started to pray for the day. That's when the Lord gave me a vision.

Thank goodness I wasn't driving!

> *In the vision, I saw Peter at work at NBC. He was walking down the hall where he saw Brandon—who approached Peter and asked him to come into his office.*
>
> *Once inside, Brandon said, "Peter, I have an idea for a television show. I want you to produce it. It's centered around children in their classroom and focuses on the everyday life and challenges that students face."*

I was quite excited, to say the least! I turned to Peter and said, "I just had a vision from God. Today, you will run into Brandon in the hallway at NBC."

Before I could continue, Peter was shaking his head in disbelief.

I tried to go on, but Peter said, "Nope, you're wrong. You are not hearing from God."

I replied with surprise, "I don't know what you're saying. Please let me finish."

Once again, Peter shook his head and said, "Connie, I will not see Brandon in the hall today. He had plans to leave last night for Europe and will not be back for two weeks."

I continued on. "Peter, you definitely will see Brandon in the hall today. He will ask you to come into his office and he will present an idea to you. It's just like the dream God gave me that night—with children in a classroom."

Seeing that I was getting nowhere, I left Peter's car to get into mine and headed back for home. I joyfully sang out to him, "Call me after your meeting with Brandon."

On the way home, I thanked God for the vision that He gave me. Once at home, I waited in anticipation of the phone call.

Since I was active on our children's school board, it was my job to prepare the agenda for an upcoming event. With notebooks on the kitchen table, I was ready to dig in when the phone rang. It was Peter.

> *"Connie, you won't believe this! I was walking down the hall and there was Brandon! I was truly shocked to see him, and asked him why he was here. After he explained to me that his trip to Europe had been canceled, he asked me into his office, where he shared an idea for a television show. He said everything just as God showed you! Children in elementary school."*

After the exhilarating conversation, I stopped to thank God and made known my appreciation and sheer excitement over the events of the morning.

In a turn of events, the contract was made for *Good Morning Miss Bliss,* and the show was sold to the Disney Channel. Everything remained the same at NBC—we simply became family with Disney as well.

Writers were hired, locations booked, and now it was time for casting the teacher, *Miss Bliss*. Haley Mills became everyone's choice to play the part. She was charming and we loved her. We were thrilled when she accepted the part.

After the children were cast, the production started and the first show was taped. I remember sitting next to Brandon, who wore a proud look on his face, as the audience wildly applauded.

Part of God's dream had become a reality. Now I wondered how this would someday turn into teens in high school.

Good Morning Miss Bliss was quickly a success, but Brandon intervened and went one step further. Yes! *Teens in high school.* So the plans began and a contract was made with NBC for a new show. The kids in Miss Bliss were now in high school, and we changed the title to *Saved by the Bell.*

This show was certainly a success. The cast was truly talented and the crew, amazing. Everyone made this show work—and for many, many years.

Not only were we blessed with *this* show, but we later developed five other shows for children and teens.

Now not only did our own children have something good to watch on Saturday mornings, but children in over eighty-five countries, as well.

When something comes from the throne room of Heaven, it will succeed and bring forth fruit. And only God deserves the glory.

How blessed we were to be a part of God's plan. To have heard His voice and His direction. Thankfully, we were willing to do what He asked of us. He gave us more than we could have dreamed of. What an awesome God we serve!

CHAPTER EIGHTEEN

Nippy

I cringed, as I witnessed the small creature lie still. Would God actually heal this animal? Would God mend my young son's broken heart? I could only hope and pray that He would.

Bringing up children without pets is leaving out a lot of love and adventure for them to enjoy. But in our case, we had no choice. I had an allergy condition that hindered us from having pets in our home. Somehow, goldfish didn't fill the gap.

A friend called one day, asking if we could take her bunny, Snowfur. She was moving and couldn't keep him any longer. I explained my problem to her, but she insisted that Snowfur was quite content living outdoors in a cage.

I thought of my boys, how they adored animals. I agreed to take Snowfur. He'd live outside.

Joshua and Stephen were delighted beyond words with the thought of having a little, sweet rabbit, to cuddle and take care of. They could hardly wait to receive their new pet.

When my friend arrived with the white, furry, ball of delight, the looks on the boy's faces were worth it. They handled him so very gingerly and laughed affectionately at his every move.

After a week of getting used to the new member of our family, I became aware of his aging. He wasn't as young as I had first believed he was. The thought of losing him so soon after adopting him was sobering. I grabbed the boys, and we were off to the pet shop. Snowfur needed some company.

I had no idea that the company would end up being four more rabbits! We quickly put together the cages for Snowfur's new friends.

Joshua and Stephen named three of the rabbits, leaving the fourth one for Lauren, their half-sister, to name. Upon her arrival for summer break, she took one look at the nameless bunny and said, "*Noonan*." Everyone was pleased.

Having new pets turned out to be a good learning tool for the children. They felt they had responsibility for something other than themselves.

Although Snowfur was aging quickly, he still had his spunk. Valentine was a larger rabbit, who had silky, black fur with large patches of white. Tinkerbell was the explorer—always straying off. Noonan had a mind of his own and loved eating everyone's food. Last but not least—the one loved by all—Nippy. He was the most affectionate of the five pets.

One sunny spring day, our nephew, Carl, was coming over to visit. He was truly excited to see the boys and to meet their new pets.

Not long into the visit, though, an accident occurred. The bunnies were let loose onto the bricks in the backyard, where we were sitting. It was fun to see Joshua and Stephen showing them off to their older cousin.

Joshua started to skip around the bricks trying to encourage Nippy's follow. Just when I was about to caution Joshua that bunnies are different than puppies, his left foot came down heavily to meet with Nippy's tender, small body.

A shrilling scream came from my son. Nippy was laying there—his body helplessly jerking. It was apparent that there was neurological damage to this dear, little creature.

Everyone started to panic. Joshua immediately ran up to his room, while shouting of how he had killed his little bunny, and that he hated himself.

At my request, Peter ran quickly to get me a towel. I gently wrapped it around Nippy and headed upstairs to Joshua's room. I knew how vitally important it was for Joshua to have closure with his pet. He could hardly look at him.

After prayer with Joshua, I left in my car with the bunny in the seat beside me, and headed for the emergency pet hospital.

I placed my hand on Nippy and prayed to God:

"Heavenly Father, I am in such pain for my son! His heart is broken at the thought of killing his own pet. He is far too sensitive a child to endure this kind of torture. Please heal his broken heart, and don't let him suffer with this enormous guilt. I pray for Nippy—this innocent, little bunny—that You would miraculously heal him and take any pain away from him. In Jesus' name, I pray."

Immediately at the end of my prayer, Nippy—who had been motionless—moved his position on the car's seat. This gave me hope.

I parked and carefully carried Nippy into the animal hospital. The kind receptionist saw the severity of his state, and hastily led us into an examination room.

The veterinarian came in, took one look at Nippy, and expressed hopelessness for him. I told her that I was believing for a miracle and had been praying continually since the accident happened. She took him to the X-ray room. I waited and prayed.

When the doctor re-entered the room, she had a smile on her face, and said, "You won't believe this, but when we were about to take an X-ray of your bunny—he sat right up and looked at us!'

Placing the X-ray over the light, she pointed-out that Nippy's skull had been crushed. He also had several broken ribs and encountered extreme neurological damage—but was absolutely fine.

The X-ray showed that the skull and the ribs had been mended as if they were old injuries that had healed. She admitted that this was a miracle.

On the drive home, I kept imagining the expression on Joshua's face when he would see a healed Nippy. Because God so loves the children, He shows His compassion in their time of suffering. Thank you, Jesus!

CHAPTER NINETEEN

Princess Child

God's ways are beyond our understanding. These supernatural events brought deep healing and reconciliation to a family—and beauty from ashes.

Looking for schools in Los Angeles takes a substantial amount of time and patience. When my son, Joshua, was born, the furthest thing from my thoughts was which school he would attend.

By the time Joshua was two years old, other parents with children the same age were talking about how crowded all of the preschools were. It wasn't long before I realized the effort it would take finding the right educational institution.

So the search began. A friend told me about a preschool that was located near my neighborhood. Without hesitation, I made an appointment. Not wanting to make a wrong decision concerning Joshua's future, I prayed for clarity.

By the look on the director's face, as she interviewed Joshua, I had no doubt that he would be accepted into the school.

Two years into Sunny Preschool, Joshua's younger brother was at the age to participate. We once again applied. Stephen also found favor and was accepted.

After preschool, we wanted to find an elementary school with good values. I looked over the small written list of schools we had collaborated from word-of-mouth suggestions. I remembered a certain day, years ago.

When Joshua was a mere month old, we had an enjoyable visit from my mom and dad. It was a breathtaking afternoon with a light breeze and we decided to go for a ride. Venturing our way up into the nearby hills, we came upon a lovely sign which read the name of a school. Something about the sign impressed me, and as the school came into our view, I could see why. It was as though we were in Connecticut. It just didn't look like L.A.

Traveling along the narrow road, we drove parallel to a white, ranch-style fence which ran along the front of the property. Behind the fence were charming, white cottages with French windows and doors. A sprawling brick patio led to paths which joined with emerald green grass and trees that seemed to smile at you.

We all gasped as we saw the stunning view from the hill the school stood upon. It embraced the sight of Los Angeles and the ocean all in one. It seemed like a dream to me, and I was hopeful that it was an elementary school.

Then to my joy, I saw small chairs inside the classrooms. It certainly looked like the right environment for my Joshua. We applied to the school on the hill and to another competitive school, as well. We had learned that hundreds of families were turned away yearly because of the huge demand. I then did the very thing I should have done the first day of school-hunting. I got down on my knees and prayed.

From that point on, I felt secure. I knew that the Lord was in charge, and that I could simply cruise along by faith and follow His instructions.

Six months later, not to my surprise, Joshua was accepted into both of the private schools.

Now, another decision had to be made, but my husband and I were confident that the Lord would show us which school to choose.

So once again, prayer was sent up with expectation of an answer before the schools' acceptance deadlines arrived.

Later, while praying in my bedroom, I heard the awesome voice of our dear Lord. He told me that we were to enroll Joshua into the school on the hill and that He would use me there for *His* purposes.

A few years later, both of our sons were at the school. This is when I met Kandy, the new receptionist.

Kandy was about five feet five inches tall, with dark, cropped hair and always presented a charming smile. She was truly polite and very responsible, as she bounced around from office to office. This awarded her favor in the eyes of everyone. I knew she'd be there for a long time.

While getting to know Kandy, I discovered a shy character that was hidden under her vibrant countenance. I learned that she had been a child princess in her native land. Her mother had died when Kandy was quite young, and her father had abandoned her a short time later. Consequently, she was raised by foster parents until she was adopted.

Toward the end of our tenure at the school, I served as president of the Parents' Club, therefore, frequently called the school and spoke to Kandy.

It was her job to type up announcements and scheduled events in the school's newspaper—along with assisting the Board. This was how we grew to be close.

Our friendship was enhanced when we found out that we were both Christians. We prayed together on the phone regardless of how busy Kandy was—as she always made time for prayer.

Kandy had two children. Jenny, who attended the school, and James, who attended school elsewhere. Kandy's husband, Dan, spent most of his time working outside of the country, which left Kandy living as a single parent. She persevered and succeeded as a good mother and provider for her children, while striving to obtain the best for them.

Years passed, and Joshua was attending the sixth grade, and Stephen, the fourth. This was a great year for all of us—until one morning when I received a phone call. It was from the headmaster of the school, John Marks. I had no idea that *this* phone call would change my life dramatically over the next two years.

It was a beautiful morning. The air still embraced a sweet smell of summer—as fall shyly approached. I awoke early, got the boys off to school, and organized my day.

While checking my long list of errands and appointments, the phone rang. I grabbed the receiver and sang-out an ambitious, "Hello!"

The responder was not as ambitious as I, and proceeded to inform me of some very disturbing news. John explained the detrimental state of health of our mutual friend, Kandy. He told me that her cancer, from years ago, came back and had settled in her lungs and liver.

The word, "liver," was the last thing I heard. I began to sob loudly into the phone and cried, "Oh no! God, please help us!"

John also cried. He asked if I'd pray, and informed me that Kandy had confided in him. He didn't feel it was appropriate for me to tell her that I knew anything at this time. He simply wanted me to begin praying for her.

I sat at the kitchen table and collected my thoughts. I recalled that Kandy had shared with me of having cancer while in her twenties. She was now in her early thirties.

I had learned that the chance of cancer returning to a woman who had breast cancer in her twenties was enormous—and could possibly return to the lungs or liver, or both. At that point, the prognosis was very poor.

Remaining at the kitchen table for hours, I prayed and read Scripture, while pleading for Kandy. I asked God to put it on her heart to call me.

Because of my respect for John and my own conscience, I certainly couldn't mention to Kandy that I knew about her cancer returning.

Still pleading with God to bring her to me, so that I'd have an entrance to help her, I yearned to put my arms around Kandy and comfort her.

I was still at my position, not wanting to move until I heard from Kandy—but soon, I had to leave for carpool. On my way to the school, I missed the turn for the carpool lane, so had to park and walk in to get my sons. I sat in my car in front of the school and waited to hear the dismissal bell. After a minute or two, I saw with my peripheral vision, a car slowly pulling up beside me. I heard a voice call my name. I lifted up my sulking face, and to my utter amazement—there was Kandy!

I jumped out of my car and climbed into Kandy's, as I heard her timid voice say:

"Connie, please help me!"

A second later, I grabbed her into my arms. We held a tight embrace as we wept together. Not one car passed us or honked to get around. God gave us a special moment in time.

Kandy shared all of what John Marks had told me, and then looked into my eyes with expectation. She hoped that I could give her a reason, an answer.

"Connie, they gave me five months to live."

Determined to stay strong, I boldly prayed for a miraculous healing for Kandy. After the prayer, she said: "Okay, I'm healed!"

A day did not come and go without my calling Kandy, whether at school or at her home. I knew of every appointment, test, and result. She kept believing—and I kept praying. But when I would pray for my dear sister, I would hear the same thing every time: *"This will come to death."*

I argued with the Lord and begged for Him to heal Kandy, but would still hear those words many times again. I honestly couldn't understand God, concerning her. I asked Him repeatedly of why she would die so young with two children to raise and a husband far away.

A Scripture then came to mind explaining that God's ways are higher and different than ours.

Kandy's faith was so incredible! At times, I felt as though it was my fault she hadn't been healed. Maybe I didn't have enough faith. Was I getting in the way of her healing? But I soon realized my foolishness. After all, God is the author of life and death. He has everything in *His* control.

During the next year, Kandy would periodically come to my home on Thursday mornings to attend my women's prayer group. We would all agree together in prayer for Kandy's healing.

From the time of her diagnosis, I never once told Kandy what God had shared with me. Who was I to crush her faith? It was the very thing that enabled her to live. I awaited God to show me how and when I could help her.

Kandy was going to work about twice a week for a time, but now was showing up every two weeks—only when she wasn't nauseated or weak.

When I called Kandy at home, I would occasionally speak to her children, Jenny and James. I could tell that their mother's demise was far from their thoughts.

At times, I would leave messages telling Kandy how much everyone loved and missed her while encouraging her to stay close to the Lord.

I tried to convince Kandy to write a letter to each of her children. She couldn't believe I would ask her to do such a thing—while believing in her heart that she would be healed. Her response to me was precise: "Connie, if I write that letter I will die. I'm not going to die!"

After pleading with God numerous times to heal Kandy—suddenly, to my surprise—I felt peaceful. No matter what God chose to do, I would trust Him.

Kandy's husband, Dan, was making the effort to come to California more often to spend time with her and the children. He would accompany Kandy to the appointments and treatments. *It never ceases to amaze me how tragedy brings people together!*

As the days carried on, Kandy would get better at times, but slip back again, soon after. She had lost all of her hair and wore scarves. A friend took her shopping for a wig, and Kandy started coming to our prayer group again.

It was hard for her to sit for two hours, and harder still to keep her balance when she walked. But Kandy was very determined and independent.

At the end of each meeting, I would make her promise me that she would call the moment she got home. She always did.

That April, things significantly worsened for Kandy—even when the test results improved. *We never could figure out those numbers!* But any number that came back lower was a praise report for us.

At her weakest moments, she began to doubt. Not with a statement or declaration of defeat, but through the tone of her voice or a hint of depression. I found myself running out of things to say to comfort her. I truly was speechless when she finally agreed to write letters to her children.

Two weeks later, Kandy gave me the letters. One for James, the other for Jenny. I directly put them in a safe place and knew they would soon be a blessing to them.

I started to speak to Kandy of heavenly things more often. Sometimes she would listen and ask questions, and other times remind me that she wasn't going to die.

A few days later, I shared a long visit with Kandy. We waited for the doctor to come and explain the latest extensive test results to us. She was happy I was with her.

After a few hours, the doctor finally came. He was short in stature, wore aqua-blue framed glasses and had a neatly trimmed beard. By the look on his face, we anticipated bad news.

He started to speak and my stomach began to knot-up while I watched Kandy's face.

Our insight proved to be correct. Kandy's cancer had spread to her female organs and bladder, as well.

When all of our questions were answered, and the doctor left, Kandy and I just stared at one another. Kandy's words to me were a witness of enormous faith:

"Yeah, but it can still be healed!"

Yes, it could still be healed, but was it God's plan to intervene and wipe the cancer cells far from Kandy?

The next day, they moved Kandy into another room. I assumed this was where they put terminally ill patients. I couldn't help but think it was odd that Kandy had never prepared her children for any of this. I tried to convince Kandy to discuss her condition and the possibility of death with them, but her answer was always the same. Her faith would not allow her to disbelieve. I admired her faith and respected her decision to remain in that place.

On my next visit, I entered a quiet, dark room carrying gifts from our school fair. The annual event was Kandy's favorite, and I knew she was sad to miss it. I brought an oversized, bright-pink poster splattered with the well-wishes and signatures of hundreds of students and their families. I quietly pinned it to the bulletin board while trying not to wake her. I arranged the gifts from students and parents on the counter next to her bed.

Slowly, I sat down on the only chair in the room. I watched her in silence. Her body was swollen and her face looked worn, yet peaceful. I felt a tear emerge and found myself fighting back more before they came.

I wondered if I should stay. Was I going against Kandy's will, since she had requested no visitors that day? I wondered if she meant *me* as well.

To honor her desires, I decided to leave. Quietly, I picked up my belongings and headed for the door. Behind me, her voice followed, as a soft whisper. "Hi."

I turned, partly wishing she hadn't awakened, thinking she would be unhappy with me. But a small smile visited her parched lips. She asked me to moisten them for her. I took out my gloss stick and gently rolled it over the dryness.

After showing Kandy the poster and gifts, I asked her if she would like for me to leave or for me to sit quietly praying, as she slept.

"Stay," she said.

I continued to pray silently for Kandy. After about twenty minutes, I moved the chair over by her side. I sang worship songs and held her hand. As I sang, tears rolled down her cheeks onto the hard, plastic pillow. The individual tears joined together and became streams.

I realized then, that Kandy had faced her mortality. She knew she would soon meet with death. I leaned over and kissed Kandy on the forehead and told her how much I loved her.

"Go home," she said sweetly.

The following day, I came to see Kandy after carpool. There was a change in her for the worse. She could hardly speak.

I sensed a sudden urgency to make some phone calls. I got in touch with John and pleaded with him to take Kandy's children out of school and bring them to see her. I explained that I felt Kandy had a small amount of time left and that her children should be with her now—until the end.

I asked Kandy for her brother's phone number. She said it was in her address book in the drawer under the tray table. I called the number and Kandy's brother answered. I explained that time was short, and suggested the family may want to come visit Kandy before it was too late. He agreed and said he'd start making plans.

I also mentioned that I would like to reach Kandy's biological father. He gave me a number, and in less than a minute, I had him on the phone. After inhaling deeply, I told him of Kandy's condition.

"Do you think she wants to speak to me?" he asked.

I answered *yes* and proceeded to put the phone up to Kandy's ear. She spoke softly and with great sincerity:

"Dad, I love you."

Her father apparently said the same thing back to Kandy. She couldn't talk any longer, so I spoke to her father for a moment. With great emotion, he told me that Kandy had never told him that she loved him. He wept.

When Kandy's children arrived, she seemed to perk up and feel better. *What an incredible show*, I thought—knowing how difficult this was for her. We stood around Kandy's bed when she gave me a look, as though to say, "It's time."

She asked me to take the kids down the hall for a cola. I knew exactly what she meant. She wanted for them to know.

The walk down the hall was of great difficulty for me. When we got our drinks and sat down, I told Jenny and James about their mother—that she was going to die. To my surprise, there were no tears from James, but plenty from Jenny.

We discussed the situation for quite a while. James asked an extraordinary amount of questions. I knew I couldn't possibly answer them all, so promised that I would see Kandy's oncologist with him soon.

The children decided to ask their father to make the long trip out. They made their call.

It was overcast the next day, as though, it was a reflection of my own heart—clouded with sadness.

I waited in the hall, while a couple of close friends from school visited with Kandy. While overhearing some of their conversation, I realized that many people thought that I had lost my mind—that I had plenty of nerve calling all of Kandy's family—stirring up panic. They also commented on how much time I had spent there with Kandy's children. *After all, they saw how good Kandy looked.*

Whenever a visitor came to see Kandy, she sat up in bed, smiled, and even cracked jokes. I loved her for this. I knew God's timing was soon, and that I had to appear as a fool for the Lord's plan.

The next day, Kandy's father and brother arrived. Her father was an older man with a gray mustache which took on the shape of a butterfly when he smiled. Her brother was a tall man with a healthy head of dark hair and a calming demeanor. Also joining them, were some relatives who traveled a long distance.

By this time, Kandy could hardly open her eyes, and was not able to calculate how many people were in the room. Her coloring was yellow, which was enhanced by the billowing yellow curtains covering the large bay window next to her bed.

Kandy's brother came into her room and gently spoke her name. Her eyebrows twitched. She opened her eyes and stared into his face. The same happened when her father spoke. She knew they were there.

Before I left, late that afternoon, Kandy had slipped into unconsciousness. I asked the family, the nurse, and the social worker to hold hands and stand around Kandy's bed.

I prayed with them, that the Lord would be so kind to take Kandy gently and peacefully *home*. I thanked Him for allowing all of her family to be able to see her—and especially to talk with her on the phone two days before. I thanked God for Kandy and her precious life—and how her life has genuinely affected ours. I asked God to prepare our hearts to say goodbye, and then dedicated her to the Lord. We silently stood around her bed in an atmosphere of total peace.

I knew that Kandy's husband would arrive shortly, and would stay by her side.

While leaving the room, I knew that I had just seen Kandy for the last time—and that I wouldn't see her again until Heaven.

On the drive home from the hospital, I reflected on the last few weeks and how challenging they had been. I thought of all the prayers that my young, believing sons sent up for Kandy. Would they be discouraged by her death? Would they learn that not all prayer is answered the way we think—or hope it should be?

I reflected on the time that I quickly jumped out of my car to get to Kandy. How strong she was in confessing her faith for healing. The many times we prayed and cried together on the phone. *I would miss her terribly!*

As I pulled into the driveway and opened the garage door, I saw my son, Joshua. His darling face, peering out the door, as he awaited my arrival. The greeting was such comfort for one who felt so weary. Shortly, my precious son, Stephen, arrived at the door. Soon, I was smothered with kisses and engulfed with hugs. *I thanked the Lord for my two gifts!*

On my bed that night, I read the Bible and offered prayers for Kandy and her family. I thanked God that Dan was there to hold Kandy's hand. I prayed that somehow the peace of God would prevail in their broken hearts. I also prayed for preparation for *my* family as well. I was absolutely exhausted and slept peacefully until I was awakened by a presence in the room.

I glanced at the clock. It read 4:50 AM. My eyes were then drawn toward a figure walking around in the middle of my bedroom. The figure was in the shape of a tall, thin man, and glowed as lightning. It brought me comfort and peace.

I was distracted when the phone rang. I looked at the clock to see it was 5:00 AM.

It was Dan. With a sorrowful tone, he told me that Kandy had died ten minutes ago.

It was the same time the angel appeared in my room!

Once we hung up, I thanked the Lord for sending me a comforter at the exact time of Kandy's death. I felt loved and cared for. This also made it easier for me to sit up and call John. I calmly searched for John's phone number.

It took two rings and John answered the phone. I told him Kandy had died just moments ago. He thanked me for calling him early, so he'd have time to inform the faculty and staff before the students arrived. He was very appreciative and told me he'd speak to me later that day.

After our conversation, I recalled a hint of surprise in John's voice. No one seemed to be prepared for the timely approach of Kandy's death—except for me. And *I* only knew because of the Lord's gracious prompting.

Before, while anticipating Kandy's upcoming death, I had suggested to her brother to look into funeral arrangements. Even though he seemed surprised at my suggestion, he complied. So when Kandy died that next day, the funeral home had already been notified.

They planned an evening service to be held so that all of Kandy's friends from school could participate.

One thing I didn't expect to do, was to speak at Kandy's funeral. I was pleasantly surprised when her brother, Brandy, asked me if I would. Of course, I said, yes.

I sat at my computer to write what I'd say on that emotional day. The words weren't coming. I bowed my head and asked for guidance. When I finished, I had no doubt that I had heard from God. This is what I spoke:

"The most precious and unique gift that Kandy had was the ability to put others before herself. When I would call to check-in with her to ask about the result of a blood test, she would put that aside and ask if my son, Joshua, made the baseball team—or how Stephen did on his math test. Then, she would talk about herself briefly, only to give me hope—even if there were a negative report.

Kandy grew emotionally and spiritually while she was dying. I will quote a cripture from 2 Corinthians, 4:16-18: 'Therefore we do not lose heart, but though our outer man is decaying, yet our inner man is being renewed day by day.'

I've never known a woman of such faith and strength. In 2 Timothy, 4:7, it says: 'I have fought the good fight, I have finished the course, I have kept the faith.'

In Psalm, 27:13,14, it reads: 'I would have despaired unless I had believed that I would see the goodness of the Lord in the land of the living. Wait for the Lord; Be strong, and let your heart take courage; Yes, wait for the Lord.'"

Written below is the prayer I shared with the congregation:

"Father, we are together, in one accord, to thank You for sharing your daughter, Kandy, with us. We thank You for her friendship, her strength, and her love.

We pray that You will watch over her children, James and Jenny—guiding them and instilling your ways into their hearts. Teach them to trust in You. Help them to remember and to put forth all of the good morals, values, goals, and dreams their mother shared with them. Draw them close to You at this time of their great sorrow, and then turn their sorrow into laughter—their mourning into joy at the appropriate time.

Bless Jenny and James, and all of Kandy's family with peace that surpasses understanding, with hope to go on, and grace to endure all things. May they reap the blessings from all of the good seed Kandy had sown.

Lord, thank You that You enabled us to stay strong in your strength for Kandy this past week and a half. Your timing was perfect in the uniting of relationships. The forgiveness and expressions of love that took place between Kandy and her family, were truly divine.

I thank You, along with everyone here tonight, for the gift You gave us in Kandy. She was a treasure to all of us. And now what better place could Kandy be—than with You, in her glorified body in Heaven forever and ever. In Jesus' name, Amen."

After I gave Jenny and James the letters from their mother, I drove home. I wondered if they would ever be the same. Could they become better people from this? One question after another popped into my head until I was so overcome with emotion that I had to come to a stop—and cry.

One afternoon, I received flowers. To my surprise, they were from Kandy's biological father. The letter attached contained such blessing that I read it several times. He graciously thanked me for all that I had done for Kandy and her family. But the most wonderful part of the letter was when he spoke of God. He expressed that because Kandy said that she loved him, he had dedicated his life to God—and was even going to read the Bible.

Love indeed conquers all! The Lord was merciful to have divinely arranged the conversation that day—when Kandy spoke those life-changing words to her father. Words that she could never have imagined saying. He now loves God and desires a close relationship with Him because of the forgiveness and love that had flowed through his daughter—in her moment of death.

When I grieve over the loss of Kandy, I reflect on the fruit that came from her death. Kandy's relationship with her real father was healed after more than thirty years of non-existence—*and* he received the Lord. Her adopted father also came to know Jesus as Lord. Dan lovingly reunited with his children. I learned to be more sensitive to the Holy Spirit's guidance, as He led me through the last two years of Kandy's life. Many relationships were healed and prayers were answered. My boys, Joshua and Stephen, also had seen God's hand move in mighty ways.

The most wondrous thing of all, is what we learned about life and death—that in a very mysterious way—they are one.

CHAPTER TWENTY

The Generator

The word of knowledge is a spiritual gift listed in the Bible. This gift is used for many purposes. To heal, restore, encourage, warn—and in some cases—save lives.

I love this gift from God and am so happy that He has generously given it to me. Through the years, I have seen wonderful things because of God's word for someone. I am grateful and give Him all the glory.

Something I didn't know, was that my son, Joshua, would have this gift—until one day during a trip to New York.

We were on our way to attend the wedding of Joshua and Stephen's older cousin. The boys were excited as we packed the night before, making sure we had everything we needed. For Stephen, this meant a lot of items to keep him busy. Puzzles to drawing materials all came along. I noticed Joshua slipping in a large bag of M&M's as he looked up and gave me a wink.

We went to bed early to be rested for our journey. I reflected on Psalm 91:11, which reads:

"For He will give His angels charge concerning you, to guard you in all your ways."

I asked God to put angels around our plane and take us to New York safely.

It was still dark outside when my alarm clock sang out at 5:30 AM. *Time to get things going!* Everyone was excited to go to the airport, so by 6:30 AM, we had all showered, eaten, and were out the door.

While on the freeway, we discussed who would sit with whom. My husband and I took turns sitting with the boys so we could always have equal, quality time with both of them.

Stephen wanted Daddy, so that was that. Once we were parked, Peter quickly put Stephen's paper and pens and small books into his own carry-on. Joshua had his school backpack readied on his shoulders.

I loved sitting next to Joshua on a plane. We always had endless conversations about our kindred interests. Because of this, our trips always seemed to be quick to deliver us to our desired destination.

Waiting in our seats, Joshua and I gazed outside and watched the crew perform their final check on the plane next to us. Joshua asked me about the generator on our plane.

I asked him why he wanted to know about the generator—and thought it was peculiar of him to ask about it.

"I don't know," Joshua answered. "I don't even know what a generator is, but I was just curious about it. Is there a big one or several of them, or what?"

I really had no clue, so I simply answered, "I don't know about the generator on a plane. It would be interesting to find out."

Once on the tarmac, we forgot about the generator and were readying for take-off. I felt pretty relaxed, considering my dislike of flying. Joshua and I prayed for the flight.

After being in the air for about an hour, Joshua and I noticed the lights on the plane flickering. We started feeling warm, as though the air vents had stopped working. Joshua looked nervous, which in turn made me feel the same way. He whispered, "Mom, what's going on with the lights?"

Before I could answer, the plane shifted into a significantly lower speed. I took my son's hand and said, "I think we'd better start praying, honey."

We began to pray just as the pilot's voice blared over the speaker system.

"Ladies and gentlemen, girls and boys, I guess you've wondered why we're turning around. We've had some difficulty with our flight. It seems that our main *generator* is not working. We will try and land in Las Vegas. Please relax and we'll let you know how it goes."

My heart seemed to skip a beat, as I recalled how serious the pilot's voice sounded. Looking around at the other passengers, I realized that they were feeling the same way.

With desperate expression, I looked back at my husband, who surprisingly was oblivious to the entire ordeal. In a serious voice, I said to him, "Did you hear that?"

To my absolute amazement, he answered: "Boy, it sure is a good thing we didn't tell my family we'd make it to the rehearsal dinner."

I glanced at Stephen and wanted to grab him in my arms, but didn't want to alarm him. Joshua and I moved very close together and continued to pray diligently. I could feel his precious hands shaking in mine—his pulse pounding through his fingertips. We prayed a profound prayer in each other's arms:

"Lord, hear our cry! Please spare our family and all the passengers on this plane. We ask You

have mercy upon us and protect us from any harm. We pray that You would fix this generator yourself. Please, God, save us!"

Fifteen minutes passed when we noticed the lights flicker back on. The pilot's voice was heard:

"Well, ladies and gentleman, girls and boys, it looks like we'll be going on to New York after all. Our generator has somehow fixed itself. We've had a miracle!"

Joshua and I hugged in celebration. I looked back at Peter and Stephen. As my husband would put it, he was again oblivious. I grabbed Stephen's hand in mine and told him I loved him. I then looked at Joshua and said, "Sweetheart, our prayers worked. God heard our cry!"

I sat peacefully and explained to Joshua how his inquiry about the generator, at the beginning of the flight, was actually a word of knowledge. And now that he has experienced this, he can recognize it next time and pray.

Joshua brought out his bag of M&M's, gave me a grin and said, "Now we *really* have something to celebrate. Dig in!"

As we prepared to have our snack, I remembered the prayer that I had said the night before—asking for God to put angels around our plane.

Realizing the angels were already positioned around the plane, I understood how they could fix the generator so quickly.

"Thank You, God! My caring, wonderful God."

CHAPTER TWENTY-ONE

The Dream that Came True

God gives dreams to His children at times we least expect them. These dreams are always very clear and are delivered with great peace—even when they come with a warning. God revealed to me an upcoming event that would take place concerning an old friend. As I waited on the Lord, that dream became a reality—one that was hard to live-out. When I was in my early twenties, I met my friend, Ricky and his wife, Leslie, through some mutual friends from England. One evening, they invited me to their home for dinner. Upon arriving, I noticed that their house resembled an authentic country-cottage.

Ricky greeted me with a welcoming smile. He was clothed with a starchy-white shirt loosened to the second button. A chocolate brown dinner jacket settled atop forest-green trousers. White socks peeked between the trousers and leather loafers which were firmly planted on the entry hall of their lovely home.

The great room exploded with intricate fabrics that covered the oversized sofas and chairs. The lighting was soft, yet able to highlight every inch of space. The ceiling towered over the sand-toned hardwood floors that cleverly showcased the brightly painted colors of the room.

Leslie took great care in designing their abode with her exquisite taste—and her own beauty was to be admired. I stayed focused on her eyes. They were so skillfully shaped with the most unusual color I had ever seen. A subtle lavender with blue tones that danced when she spoke. The black and gold silk blouse she wore was uniquely harmonious with her creamy-white skin and jet-black hair. While we sat at the rustic bar, glittering with Waterford crystal on their stems, she smiled at me. I felt we would be friends forever.

Years passed, and many fond memories were made, and milestones were achieved in our friendship. I would please dear Ricky by listening to lengthy stories of his childhood adventures in Maine—and would eagerly partake of the gourmet dinners, Leslie generously labored over. But before long, we lost touch.

One day, though, I was driving through a picturesque neighborhood and spotted a car that looked like Leslie's dusky-gray sedan. It pulled up alongside of my jet-black jeep. Emotions flurried, as I tried to see who the driver was. Surprisingly, the driver noticed me too. When she looked over, the late morning sunlight brought her face to view. I could tell it was indeed, Leslie. Right away, she moved over to the side of the road under a blossoming Jacaranda tree, and eagerly motioned for me to do the same.

Once parked, I noticed two car seats in the back of her car. It was apparent they were for the son and daughter she had during the years of our break in friendship. As I approached them, sliding through lavender petals like snow on the ground, she maneuvered her daughter over to the window. By the time I got there, she had placed the child in my arms.

Leslie had missed our friendship, and it grieved her that I hadn't been there for her most prized moments—the birthing of both Anna and Eric.

Not too long after our reunion, I received a desperate phone call from Leslie.

"Ricky's sick, Connie," she said. "Please help me through this!"

After multiple tests and several opinions, the doctors discovered that Ricky had cancer. Surgery was planned right away. I committed myself to be by Leslie's side.

My most vivid memory on the day of the surgery was of Leslie and her family hearing the frightening words the surgeon spoke:

"Ricky's cancer was worse than we thought. It has spread, but with treatment, he may have ten years left to live."

I insisted on driving Leslie home. She appeared pale and weak. My heart tightened with grief for her and the children.

After a few years, our friendship had grown a bit distant again. I started to see the pattern of weak communication. It brought forth lapses of time between each season of our treasured gatherings.

During this particular lapse, I had my two precious sons, Joshua and Stephen, and was joyfully caught up with taking care of them.

Leslie also had family responsibilities that kept her away from much socializing. I had heard that she and Ricky divorced. I prayed lengthy prayers for Leslie and the children, as well as for Ricky—always calling him on special occasions.

One December morning, God gave me a dream. In my dream, I was sitting at my desk. Upon sorting through the mail, I opened an invitation that read: *"Come to a Marriage Dinner."*

Next, in the dream, my husband and I were at *that* dinner. Ricky was the groom. I questioned a friend as to why Ricky's face was so red. He explained that Ricky's cancer had come back and the redness was a result of the rigorous radiation he was undergoing.

While eating the celebration dinner, I sensed Ricky had left the party. I looked for him, but couldn't find him anywhere—and no one knew where he had gone.

Finally, a tall, young waiter calmly told me that Ricky was in the other room, and pointed in the direction. When I took a few, short steps into that room, it became a different location. There was a small stage with a casket at center. Pews faced the still setting. I realized it was someone's funeral. When I saw Leslie and her children in the front row, focusing ahead—I knew it was a funeral for Ricky. End of dream.

Six years had gone by. It was a warm day in June and I was sitting at my desk in our small library. I shuffled through the day's mail and noticed a small envelope which was sent from Ricky. I opened it and read:

"Come to a Marriage Dinner."

It was Ricky's wedding invitation to us. It was the fulfillment of the dream that I had been given from God, all those years ago!

We attended the wedding, which was an exact representation of what I had been shown. I sadly realized that we were all going to live out that dream now—to its fruition.

By the end of September, I heard that Ricky's health was rapidly declining. I knew I needed to arrange a visit. I attempted to contact Ricky by phone numerous times, knowing that I was supposed to be of help to him. Finally, one day he answered and said he would love for me to stop by.

In diligent preparation for the visit, I sat in my living room and prayed. It was a quiet morning. My sons were in school, and no one else was in the house. Then, the Lord whispered to me and asked me to pray for *Donna*—that she would be of help to me concerning Ricky.

Although I didn't know anyone named Donna, I obediently prayed for her, as the Lord had so clearly instructed.

As I walked up the awkwardly steep driveway to Ricky's home, I prayed to God for wisdom. We sat in Ricky's bedroom. A king's-blue color of paint was the cosmetic for the walls and a white wrought-iron frame anchored his bed.

We talked about our children, and when he spoke of his, he admitted that he had been estranged from them because of the divorce. I asked Ricky if he would let me pray for him and he complied.

At the end of my prayer, Ricky's new wife, Katie, arrived with her friend—whose name was Donna! I truly couldn't believe it. Walking up the steps leading to the living room, was the person that was suppose to help me. I let the Lord lead.

The two women and I had lunch in the old-fashioned kitchen. At one point, when Katie left the room momentarily, I whispered to Donna that I had stopped by to pray for Ricky. Her mouth flew open as she gasped, and asked, "You're a believer?"

In answering her question, I shared the dream I had concerning Ricky. From that moment on we agreed to pray together.

I regularly visited Ricky, each time bringing him his favorite dishes from a local deli. We had some peaceful visits—either in his bedroom, when he was feeling weak—or in the small den, where we watched sports on TV.

During one visit, I started sharing more with Ricky about the Lord. To my disappointment, he stopped me in mid-sentence. He leaned in closely, and with his weary eyes penetrating mine, said, "Connie, I'm Jewish. I don't believe like you do."

I left that day with a sad heart.

Two weeks raced by without any visits, when I received a phone call from Donna. She told me to come quickly. After many calls for prayer support, I was on my way to the hospital.

In the small, sterile room, I saw Ricky, propped up in bed. He was unconscious and laboring for each breath. Also, in the room, were Donna, Katie, and some of Ricky's friends.

I scooted a chair close to Ricky's bed and held his hand securely for hours, as people popped in to say their last goodbyes. Nurses were scarce and a doctor would frequently come in to feed more morphine into Ricky's limp body.

I felt something urge me to go out into the hall. I followed this prompting and saw Ricky and Leslie's daughter, Anna—now a young lady. I hadn't seen her for a long period of time, but recognized her features that so reflected those of her mother.

Alongside of Anna, stood her uncle, Clark, whom I had known for many years. I told him (who showed resistance to seeing Ricky) that I would take Anna into the room to see her father. Anna told me that she was afraid to go in because of all the people who were inside. I lovingly explained how important it was that she say her last goodbye—and that if she didn't, she may later regret it.

Anna timidly walked in to see her father. I led her to the chair that I had been sitting on next to Ricky. With a break in her voice, she whispered, "Hi Daddy."

Soon after, I had an impression, once again, to go out into the hall. There, stood Eric—Ricky and Leslie's son. In like manner, I encouraged Eric, and I led him in to see Ricky.

Once I grabbed another chair, Eric sat down next to where Anna was sitting and said, "Hi Dad," in a more solid tone.

Although Ricky lay unconscious and laboring, I felt elated seeing Anna and Eric there—before their father's passing.

It wasn't long after his children's visit, when I took Donna aside. I asked if she had gotten the chance to speak or pray with Ricky before he slipped into a coma.

She said that a remarkable thing had happened. Earlier that day, she was sitting quietly at the foot of Ricky's bed. Shockingly, Ricky came out of his coma for a mere moment. Donna expressed how amazing it was, as Ricky flew-up speedily from his seemingly lifeless form into a sitting position. Then he pointed at her and demanded, "Pray for me!"

With great relief, I confidently knew my ministry with Ricky was coming to an end. I told

Donna that I sensed our mutual friend was going to die very soon, and that I didn't feel I should stay for that final departure. At first, Donna didn't want me to go, but then respected my discernment.

I flopped into my car, aching from the day's tension, and drove home through tears. I couldn't bear to sit and watch Ricky take his last breath.

Upon walking in the door of my home, the phone rang. It was Donna. She said, "Connie, ten minutes after you left the room, Ricky died."

In a brief moment, I called Leslie's home to inform her children. Anna answered the phone.

"Hi, Anna, I said. "I met you at the hospital..."

Before I could finish, Anna asked if her father had died.

I told her *yes*, and she thanked me for everything.

The next day, I got a phone call from Leslie. She said that when her daughter told her about a woman who was at the hospital—she somehow knew that Anna was referring to me.

We talked as though all the years apart accounted to nothing. She thanked me profusely for what I did for her children.

As another day came to grace us, I sat outside in my back yard, on my favorite bench, overlooking the cityscape. I appreciated the bright-white majestic clouds positioned above towering pine trees that were touching the sepia-blue sky.

I reflected on the events of the past two weeks, while feeling forever grateful for the dream God gave me that night—long ago. Because of that dream, I knew I was supposed to help Ricky during his last days.

Through this experience, I learned the profound importance of leading a person to Christ—even at the end of one's life. I witnessed how God can use even sorrowful events to bring old friends back together again.

I leaned down and picked up a smooth stone at my feet and hurled it as far as possible. Watching it eventually drop down to the ground, I thought of how short our time on earth is. And while we are here, we must do our best to make known to all in our midst, the undying love of God!

CHAPTER TWENTY-TWO

Comfort From a Painting

Adrenalin pumped through my veins, as I raced to the phone. What message would await us? Who was in danger? God, please give us strength!

Excitement whirled throughout our household, as we prepared to go to our favorite restaurant in LA. My two sons always looked forward to these special outings.

That morning, the sun was shining and all was well—except for an unexplained sadness in my heart. I knew something was happening this day that was not good.

As we carpooled to the school, I noticed Joshua's sad face in my rearview mirror. I asked, "Joshua, are you okay?" He replied, "I don't know, Mommy. I feel that something bad is going to happen."

During the course of the day, I found myself thinking of a friend of mine who had been on a downhill fight with cancer. *I wondered if he was going to die today—and that could be what Joshua and I were feeling.*

The boys arrived home. I hurried them to do their homework. Before long, their assignments were finished, and off we went.

Everything seemed so very different about *this* night. Joshua and I still felt there was something wrong. We weren't quite sure what mystery hung over us all day, but we were both experiencing the same sensations.

Once at the restaurant, my son, Stephen, and I played a game on the table with the sugar packets. It seemed to distract me for a time. Glancing over at Joshua, I could see that he was still distressed. He and I huddled together and asked God to intervene.

On the ride home, I felt the tension build. Joshua and I hadn't spoken about it since our prayers, but somehow our mutual burden was sensed by all. The second my husband parked in the driveway, Joshua and I simultaneously jumped out of the car. We headed to my small library to retrieve voice messages. With a shaky finger, I pushed the button on the phone. *The words we heard were as darts that pierced our very hearts:*

"Connie, this is a friend of Marge Bentley. Please call me at your earliest convenience."

I called back immediately and put the speaker phone on. Joshua and I stood frozen, waiting for someone to answer. Finally, someone did.

I spoke, "Hello, this is Connie. I received a message from you concerning Marge Bentley."

The woman responded, "Yes, Connie, I'm sure you're calling about the funeral arrangements."

Trembling, I hesitantly asked, "What funeral arrangements? For who?"

Embarrassed, the woman replied, "Oh, I'm so sorry, Connie! I thought you knew. Jaclyn was in a car accident this morning, and—well—she was killed."

Our friends, the Bentley's sweet daughter, Jaclyn! How could this be? She had just turned sixteen!

Joshua could hardly make it to the bathroom before becoming ill. I found myself strangled by heartbreak and tears.

My family stayed close that weekend ministering to one another. Sunday morning came and we prepared for church.

During worship, the Lord divinely graced me with a picture. My eyes closed, I saw Jaclyn in a white robe with the illuminated glory of God all around. Her face exuded an abundance of joy, which revealed her whereabouts. She was in Heaven.

I had peace throughout the day. After dinner that evening, I prayed about calling Jaclyn's family to share the vision I had. After feeling the prompting of the Lord to do so, I called.

Michael, Jaclyn's younger brother, answered with anticipation. He was the same age as my son, Joshua. They had been classmates in school until Michael moved farther north with his family. There, they thought, would be a safer place to live. They searched for a haven, hoping it would bring more quality in their lives. Ironically, not long after their move, they were planning a funeral for their daughter.

"Michael, this is Connie, Joshua's mom."

Michael knew me pretty well. We had the Bentley's over many times for barbeques and swimming. I also attended all the sport games that Joshua and Michael participated in together.

After we spoke for a while, I shared the vision I had of Jaclyn. His response was of excitement, as he pleaded with me, "Would you please paint that? Please!"

I warmly responded: "Of course I will, Michael!"

A few days later, I was on my way to the funeral. Joshua and Stephen were in school and my husband at work—so I ventured out to face this alone. I couldn't imagine how it would be to see Jaclyn's mother. *Oh, God, give me strength!*

I didn't see Marge until her dear daughter was put to rest. She was walking around the limo where her husband and sons awaited her. I stood watching quietly, not wanting to disrupt their plans—but then, she looked right at me. The second she saw me, she started to cry—a cry I've only heard from a mother who had lost a child. I ran to her and we embraced with an outpouring of emotion.

It was well into summer, as the season changes were apparent. Summer always brought great times for me and my sons. Fun in the pool and many trips to the park would be planned along with other adventures. We enjoyed short car trips, stays at resorts, and even a fishing trip.

Periodically, I would think of Jaclyn and her family. That long, heartfelt embrace with Marge. The red roses that were placed gently on Jaclyn's coffin by her young friends. And especially the vision I had of Jaclyn in Heaven.

I then remembered my promise to Michael—that I would paint that vision.

Within minutes, I was downstairs in my studio, setting up my brushes and mixing my colors. I needed to somehow portray this amazing vision onto canvas.

While painting, I'd stop many times to regain my eyesight from all of the tears giving way to my broken heart. Being a parent, I couldn't imagine what it would be like to lose a child.

In August, the portrait was finally finished. I cleaned my brushes and sat back in my rickety wooden chair to observe it one more time. *Oh, Jaclyn!*

Now to present the painting to Jaclyn's family. We made a time, and once I wrapped the painting in brown paper, we were on our way.

I remained quiet on the trip, while the boys were involved in a travel game—my husband focused on driving. Finally, we arrived at their home.

In the depth of my soul, held a place of worry. I was afraid they wouldn't like the portrait. Maybe they wouldn't think it looked like her—or that it would simply be too painful for them to view. But trying to be brave, I lifted the painting out of the car.

Jetting out of the door of their house was Michael, excited to see Joshua and Stephen, who both joined him and ran inside.

Upon entering their home, I searched for a place to put the painting until the moment of unveiling. But Thomas, Jaclyn's dad, wanted to see it immediately.

After asking the family to position themselves around the painting, I slowly unwrapped it. There was silence. Then the silence was broken as Thomas spoke: "That's my Jaclyn!"

My heart relieved, beat happily, as I went to hug Thomas, who was quietly crying.

The whole family gathered around to embrace one another, and to complement the remarkable likeness of the portrait.

It wasn't until a year later that I found out the profound effects this painting had on the Bentleys. It was early afternoon, as I was contemplating what to prepare for dinner. I looked outside to enjoy my boys shooting hoops. *Oh God, thank You for my two treasures!*

The phone rang. It was Marge. I answered and said, "Marge, it's so good to hear your voice! How are you and the guys?"

A calm voice answered, "We're doing well."

This was the best news I had heard in a year.

Marge went on to describe the unique role the portrait had in her family. She said how wonderful it was to say "hi" to Jaclyn every morning. Andy, the older brother, would look at the painting every day while saying a prayer. And Michael—*dear Michael*—would kiss Jaclyn on the cheek every night before he went to bed.

Her words were softly spoken, as she said, "Connie, you have absolutely no idea how much this painting has helped our healing process and has blessed our family!"

I reminded my friend that God gave me the vision. All I did was paint it. I thanked God and gave Him all the glory.

A painting can't bring someone back, but it's awesome what a painting can do—when it is orchestrated by the Lord!

CHAPTER TWENTY-THREE

Brandon, We Love You

Does God take control over our lives when we have lost that control? When we are in a time of deep trouble, will He rescue us?

Prayers for others will be answered, because God loves His children. On one night, in particular, our prayers were heard with powerful results!

Christmas time was approaching, as we prepared to go to Hawaii. It was a good time slot, since our sons were on winter-break from school—and Peter, on hiatus.

I missed being at home with my extended family, but soon replaced that void with our *greater* family—who also made this time their yearly tradition.

We stayed at a beautiful hotel at the end of a road where it nestled up to a private golf course. The island of Oahu is truly understated as a great getaway. The rush of tourists pacing up and down Waikiki Beach wasn't appealing to some. The small shops were now sitting in the shadows of enormous shopping centers along the main drag. But by traveling around the island away from the crowds, you would quickly realize that it is one of the most breathtaking vacation spots.

One of our most favorite indulgences was the breakfast served at our hotel. Every family had a reserved table for each morning of their stay. The environment was welcoming, along with the delectable fragrance of maple syrup. You had a view of the ocean, palm trees, and the expansive deep-blue sky. There was an excitement in the dining room as you, once again, greeted your friends to begin a new day.

After several days of relaxing on the beach, we felt refreshed. The weather was perfect this trip. We enjoyed swimming, football on the beach, and great conversations—that produced priceless bonding as a family.

Stephen's hair turned more blond with the sun, as Joshua's olive skin became more tanned. We soaked-in all of the smells and tastes this island offered.

We planned an early dinner one night, and feeling the effects of the Hawaiian sun, headed to bed early. Peter and I said our usual prayers and were fast asleep. But this was not a normal night for either of us.

Peter had three dreams—waking me up each time to share them. In each dream was Brandon Tartikoff (the president of NBC Entertainment, and also a good friend).

In the first dream, Peter and I were socializing with Brandon at a party. Then suddenly, Brandon disappeared for a while. When he came back, he said, "Don't leave me! Stay by me! Be with me!"

This same dream repeated itself.

After the third dream, I knew that Brandon was in trouble. Not knowing where he was, or what he was enduring—I prayed this prayer:

"Oh, God, please hear our cry for Brandon. I pray that if he's ill or has been in a car accident, or whatever tragedy he and his family are facing—that You will be with him, save him, and heal him. In Jesus' name."

I repeated this prayer throughout the night. Then, Peter and I started interceding together. We prayed until the early morning light shown through the drapes and the children came running into our room. We were both exhausted and filled with dire concern for our friend, Brandon.

Once we had eaten our breakfast, we settled on the beach, along with Joshua and Stephen. Around mid-morning, a hotel employee sought after us to deliver a telegram from NBC.

Our eyes magnetically met and we began to read the dreaded news.

The sender of the telegram proclaimed that Brandon Tartifkoff and his daughter, Calla, had been in a car accident the day before. His wife, Lilly, had been told that they may not make it through the night. They did somehow survive and were both in intensive care today. Calla's condition was very serious. They asked us to please pray for our NBC family. (To think that God had us praying all night!)

Years before, Brandon fought a long battle with cancer—and now he faced a war.

I couldn't control my emotions, therefore we gathered our towels and belongings—held our sons' hands—and went up to our room.

After making many phone calls, we gathered no further information than that of the original statements.

We continued in prayer for the Tartikoff's. Later, we found that Brandon was out of intensive care, but that Calla was still in very serious condition. She would soon be scheduled for brain surgery.

I kept picturing Calla's face when Brandon would bring her to our home during a party for the cast and crew of *Saved by the Bell*. She would sing, as she ran around the back yard to play. Her pretty face was an image of her handsome parents. And now, her life was in danger.

We ordered room service that night to give us more privacy so we could continue in prayer. Our sons chimed-in beautifully. I was so proud of them.

Our vacation came to an end and we were on our way back home. It was always sad to leave our special vacation place. But this time was different.

The updates on Brandon and Calla's conditions came less frequently. We believed by faith for a complete healing for them both—while also praying fervently for Lilly—knowing how stressful this tragedy must be for her.

Once home, we unpacked and went to bed early. The next day we were informed that Calla had a successful surgery, but would have difficulty from the injury to her brain.

Several years had gone by when I received a phone call from Brandon. "Connie, I heard you had surgery and I wanted to encourage you, that you will be fine." I responded, "Brandon, it is so good to hear your voice!"

We caught up a little that day, but I only saw him one more time after that. We were invited to a dinner party in Brentwood and upon our arrival, we saw Brandon. After a warm greeting, Peter and I spent some lovely time with him. He had heard that we prayed for him the night he was in the tragic accident. His gratefulness was humbling.

Not long after our reunion, we heard that Brandon's cancer had come back. Again, we started to pray daily for him.

Several months later, we were told that Brandon was in the hospital nearing his death. I invited a friend over to be with me that day. We sat and prayed for hours. As we sought the Lord, God gave me a vision.

I saw Brandon walking upward on a lit path. I realized he was going to enter Heaven. I looked at my watch to see what time this vision occurred. Ten minutes went by, and I received a phone call from a mutual friend. She said:

"Connie, Brandon died ten minutes ago."

Was I to cry or sing? To lament or rejoice? I lost an amazing friend, but gained a brother in Heaven. I will never forget Brandon Tartikoff. How he was used by God to bring forth the dream I had been given for *Saved by the Bell*. How he so tenderly called to encourage me when I was ill. Such a caring man. Such a precious soul.

Until then, Brandon.

CHAPTER TWENTY-FOUR

Miracle by the Pool

Are there really foul spirits that can control our health and well-being? Do we pray for deliverance or healing? I do know that God is faithful and will show us what to do.

Marko comes through the side gate of our property twice a week to clean our pool. He's a peaceful man, who loves the Lord and wears *that love* on his face. One morning, I was curious of why Marko carried his son on his back while he worked. It's seemingly hard enough to bend over the dazzling, blue water while keeping your balance—let alone, with the weight of a three-year-old child.

"Marko," I asked, "Is there a reason you are carrying Christopher on your back while you work so hard?"

"Yes," he answered. "Christopher isn't able to be in school yet, because he can't talk."

"Oh, I'm so sorry! Has he ever talked?"

With pained eyes, Marko looked at me and said, "No, not one word. Not one."

I gave Christopher a kiss on the cheek, and went back into my office to work on my computer, when I heard a loving voice from Heaven:

"Go and cast out the foul spirit that is in Christopher."

Needless to say—this was the voice of God. I had no choice but to obey Him and pray that a healing would take place.

As I walked up the brick steps from my office back to the pool area, I prayed that God would help me to be brave. I was concerned with hurting Marko's feelings.

I asked God for His strength, as I approached this loving father.

"Marko, may I lay hands on Christopher and pray for him?"

He instantly replied, "Yes, please do!"

Christopher looked at me with his large, brown eyes, and gave me a sweet, slight smile.

I asked this darling child if I could pray for him. He, once again, smiled at me. *That* was my answer.

Placing my left hand on Christopher, I looked straight into his eyes, and said:

"I rebuke this foul spirit in you, Christopher, and I cast it out and away from you, in Jesus' name!"

Marko looked startled. He stretched his hand around to his back. It appeared he was searching for something, then shouted out:

"Oh my Lord! I thought that Christopher had just wet his pants, because it felt so warm against my back—but it's dry."

Marko realized the warmth that he had felt was from the Lord's touch. God's healing hand on his son. He thanked me for praying, picked up his equipment—with Christopher still on his back—and went around the side of the house to leave through the gate.

I followed behind, then stood quietly at a distance. They approached the gate, and I said, "Goodbye, Christopher."

As Marko turned, so his son could see me, Christopher looked at me with a smile and said, "Bye-bye."

Those were his first words!

Marko joyfully updates me weekly at my request on Christopher's accomplishments. He's doing very well in school and making new friends. But one thing Marko told me was about himself. He said that he desires to become a pastor, and that the process of being licensed had already begun.

Because He saw God's hand on his child and witnessed the miracle of healing, he wants to serve God for the rest of his life.

There is nothing more exciting, rewarding, and peaceful, than being a part of God's Kingdom here on earth—where God uses His people—to touch His people.

CHAPTER TWENTY-FIVE

Jesus at the Gate

My prayer partners, Sarah and Jenny, were on their way over to pray. Our meeting was especially important to me. During this heartbreaking season of my life, I'd been seeking the Lord for His mercy and grace. The Lord gave me a gift that day—that I will treasure throughout eternity!

My art studio was small, but we liked meeting there weekly to pray. The structure was divided into three sections. The more spacious one was where my easel and paints were set up. Large French doors led out into a patio where there was plenty of light.

Another room, quite smaller in size, is where I stored supplies. And the third—a quaint sitting room, where I worked on my computer. This room was where we met to pray.

As I quickly cleaned my brushes, I reflected on how much time I had been spending in prayer, fasting, and seeking the Lord.

There was something I wanted from God— more of Him!

I heard a gentle knock at the door. I bounced up and greeted Sarah and Jenny. We gathered into our small corner to pray.

These two women had been precious to me for many years and had both proven to be of good character and strong women of God.

We chatted a little and then started to pray. I sat in a chair across from the loveseat they both comfortably inhabited. I bowed my head and prayed in my *prayer language*. The vision began:

Under my feet, appeared a path. This path was lit up and I followed it with my eyes. In the distance, at the end of the path, was Jesus. He stood on the threshold of the gate door which was the glorious entrance into Heaven.

As I started to walk toward Him, I glanced over to see many people behind the fence. I couldn't see the detail of their faces, but I could see their height, shape, and hair color. One woman stood out to me. I knew it was a woman I helped during the last two years of her life. Then, the revelation came:

Oh my! They are waiting there to greet me in Heaven!

I thought about searching for my dad, grandmothers, and friends—but I couldn't take my eyes off of Jesus.

He appeared to stand between six-feet to six-feet-four. His hair was brown and reached just above His shoulders. His eyes were the most beautiful eyes I had ever seen—a deep-chocolate-brown, with nothing but *love and acceptance* flowing out of them.

I walked toward Jesus, and He smiled at me. The closer I got to Him, the more He smiled—until finally all of His teeth showed. I couldn't take my eyes off of Him—and couldn't wait to get closer.

As I approached Jesus, who was standing on my right, He positioned his arms and hands the way a groom does to receive his bride.

I was excited to go into Heaven with Jesus. I reached out to allow Him to take my hands into His, but before our hands could touch—the vision stopped.

There I was, back in the small room again with Sarah and Jenny. The first thing I saw was Jenny's face, as she was sitting directly across from me. Her eyes widely opened, her mouth dropped—as she said:

"Connie, you weren't here! I mean, you were here—but I knew you were somewhere else!"

I looked at her and said, "I just saw Jesus—*face to face!*"

Both Sarah and Jenny knew that I had been somewhere else. They said my countenance was glowing and that there was silence the whole time of the vision. They just sat and watched me and waited to hear of my experience.

After telling them every detail, we joined hands, and thanked and praised God.

That night in bed, I wondered what would have happened if Jesus had taken my hands and led me over Heaven's threshold. I suppose my physical body would have died. *Poor Sarah and Jenny!*

I don't know to this day, of why I had this priceless vision, but am grateful for what it had to say to me.

I will never doubt that there is a heaven. A place to dwell forever with God. I got to see unconditional love pouring out of my Savior, and learned that my time wasn't up—I had more work to do.

> *My prayer is that all will go through that gate when they die. For me, I look forward to that day. But next time, to go over the threshold into Heaven—into the arms of Jesus.*

Afterword

If you have read this book and desire to get to know your God, I lovingly invite you into His family by saying this prayer:

Heavenly Father,
  I believe that Jesus Christ is your Son and that He died for my sins. I believe that He rose from the dead three days later, and resides with You in your throne room.
  I ask You to forgive my sins and make me whole—a new creature in Christ. I ask for the Holy Spirit to live in me, so that I may be gifted and carry on the work that You started here. Thank You for redeeming me through the shed blood of your Son.
  In Jesus' name, amen.

After you've said this prayer, I would like to encourage you to find a good church and develop fellowship with other believers. You could start reading the Bible, beginning with *The Gospel According to John*. Find a trustworthy and wise prayer partner and stay accountable to him or her. Pray without ceasing and love others as you love yourself. May God bless your journey!

And, to the believer: I hope you enjoyed hearing how God has so generously worked in my life. If you haven't already experienced the Holy Spirit in *your* life, I pray that you will be open to all that He has for you—that you will see His amazing, supernatural power and grace first-hand.

I challenge you to brave the unknown—to let go of the old, and enter into the new world of His glory. Ask the Holy Spirit to gift you and teach you about those graces that He has, especially for you. Venture out anew, into the depths of His living water—where the fish are plentiful and the blessings are without end.

About the Author

CONNIE BRYSON moved from Claremont, California to Los Angeles to pursue a career as a television commercial actress and model. While spending many years jet-setting around the world, she felt a void. That void was the absence of God in her life. In 1980, she dedicated herself to the Lord, and her life profoundly changed. She was married to Executive Producer, Peter Engel, in 1981.

Soon after, she had her two sons, Joshua and Stephen. Motherhood has been her happiest and the most fulfilling years. Connie and her husband prayed for a television show they could make for children. God blessed them with *Saved by the Bell* and other shows as well, including: *Hang Time, USA High, City Guys, Malibu, CA, One World, California Dreams, Saved by the Bell—the New Class, Saved by the Bell—the College Years,* and two television movies: *Saved by the Bell—Hawaiian Style,* and *Saved by the Bell—Wedding in Las Vegas.*

Connie also loved to paint and developed a career which landed her into several national galleries and a contract with Winn Devon Publishers. Her original photographs are displayed on the covers of this book.

She has been teaching the Bible to women for twenty-seven years, as of this publication. Connie enjoys writing, to encourage others daily, in her blog:

www.conniesencouragement.blogspot.com

Her love for God, family, and others has inspired her to share the supernatural events that God has created in her life. Connie's greatest desire is to finish well.

Also by Connie Bryson

Book Two:
The Art of Charismatic Christian Faith Series

http://www.amazon.com/MIRACLES-Inspirational-Brilliance-Charismatic-Christian-ebook/dp/B00OVLLG02

Book Three
of the Art of Charismatic Christian Faith Series

http://www.amazon.com/dp/B00VVWMUEK

Book One:
of The Art of Charismatic Christian Living Series

http://www.amazon.com/CHRISTIANS-HURTING-Charismatic-Christian-Living-ebook/dp/B00PPQ6U6M

Book Two:
of The Art of Charismatic Christian Living Series

http://www.amazon.com/COMING-TRIAL-Preparing-Charismatic-Christian-ebook/dp/B00TNYC2U0

Book Three:
of the Art of Charismatic Christian Living Series

http://www.amazon.com/HOLY-SPIRIT-COME-supernatural-Charismatic-ebook/dp/B012EODC2M

Book Four:
of the Art of Charismatic Christian Living Series
https://www.amazon.com/dp/B01KR99OVO

*Book One:
of the Art of God's Creation Series*

http://www.amazon.com/POEMS-SUMMER-Delightful-Descriptions-Creation-ebook/dp/B00W4ZO31Q

*Book Two:
of the Art of God's Creation Series*

http://www.amazon.com/dp/B010CDLTL8

Book One:
of the Art of Charismatic Christian Womanhood

http://www.amazon.com/Daughter-God-Imagining-Charismatic-Christian-ebook/dp/B01CHA3P7A

Before We Part

Dear Reader,

Thanks so very much for the time you've taken to read my book. I hope it was an inspiration to you.

Would you consider sharing something about your reading experience? Please visit this book's Amazon page and post your review there. The link:

http://www.amazon.com/MIRACLES-Something-Inspirational-Unbridled-Charismatic-ebook/dp/B00M3FV0CM

Readers all over the world benefit from comments such as yours, and I'll truly appreciate your feedback.

Blessings,
Connie

www.ingramcontent.com/pod-product-compliance
Lightning Source LLC
Chambersburg PA
CBHW071452040426
42444CB00008B/1312